WHEN MARY BECOMES COSMIC

When Mary Becomes Cosmic

A Jungian and Mystical Path to the Divine Feminine

DAVID RICHO

Paulist Press
New York / Mahwah, NJ

Front cover image: Our Lady of Vladimir, Byzantine icon. Back cover image (background) by Claudio Balducelli / Dreamstime.com.
Cover design by Tamian Wood
Book design by Lynn Else

Library of Congress Cataloging-in-Publication Data

Names: Richo, David, 1940–
Title: When Mary becomes cosmic : a Jungian and mystical path to the divine
    feminine / David Richo.
Description: New York : Paulist Press, 2016. | Includes bibliographical references.
Identifiers: LCCN 2015030246 (print) | LCCN 2015042152 (ebook) | ISBN
    9780809149827 (pbk. : alk. paper) | ISBN 9781587686023 (ebook)
Subjects: LCSH: Catholic Church. Litany of Loreto. | Mary, Blessed Virgin,
    Saint—Titles. | Mary, Blessed Virgin, Saint—Devotion to—Italy—Loreto.
    | Jungian psychology—Religious aspects—Catholic Church. | Loreto, Our
    Lady of. | Loreto (Italy)—Religious life and customs.
Classification: LCC BX2161.5.L58 R54 2016 (print) | LCC BX2161.5.L58 (ebook) |
    DDC 232.91—dc23
LC record available at http://lccn.loc.gov/2015030246

ISBN 978-0-8091-4982-7 (paperback)
ISBN 978-1-58768-602-3 (e-book)

Published by Paulist Press
997 Macarthur Boulevard
Mahwah, New Jersey 07430

www.paulistpress.com

Printed and bound in the
United States of America

For Siena, age two,
I will always see you in the arms of Mary,
Cause of Our Joy

Contents

Contents

Foreword

For centuries, Catholics have loved and honored Mary as Mother of God, and our mother. In exploring the divine feminine imaged in Mary, the author opens us to another way to honor her—not unlike the mystics, who have traveled along this way to the depths—and helps us to explore the richness that lies in what Jung referred to as the Catholic Church's treasury of image and metaphor.

This exploration is not something so esoteric that the ordinary Christian will feel lost. Quite the contrary, David Richo, gifted for making a concept like *archetype* simple and understandable, tells us it is "energy in us and in the cosmos." First, he introduces us to what he calls, the three Marys: the first Mary, the historical woman described in the New Testament as the Mother of Jesus; the second Mary, who holds the archetype of the divine feminine, expanding her meaning as an energy within us and in the world; and the third Mary, the Mary of our devotion, the Mary who is our friend and our mother, the Mary honored in the shrines where she has appeared in history. All three aspects of Mary grace us with an experience of her beauty and healing power. One way of viewing or experiencing Mary does not exclude the others.

Enriched with quotes from a variety of spiritual writers, Richo guides us through reflections on: "Who is Mary?" and "What is the divine feminine?" We have only to look at the history of humanity to note that, since the Paleolithic Period, people experienced wonder at the earth and the sky, at birth and death. Our ancestors imaged these mysteries as feminine and gradually as a Mother Divinity, Queen of Heaven and Earth. With Christianity and a masculine image of Divinity, the feminine did not disappear entirely—though the goddess did. Temples in Rome formerly honoring the pagan goddesses were renamed and dedicated to Mary, for example, St. Mary Major, a former temple to Cybele. This change, found in numerous churches throughout Christian countries indicates that the divine feminine has been honored in every age since, and that it is related to soul, to relationship, to compassion, and to healing.

The archetypal images found in the ancient and treasured Litany of Loreto form the framework for this book. In the past, we may have wondered what Mary as *House of Gold, Tower of Ivory, Mirror of Justice, Vessel of Honor,* and *Seat of Wisdom* meant. The author provides a wealth of associations to the images, all seventeen of them, enlarging and deepening our understanding. Each of these meditations is a gem; we learn, for example, that calling Mary *Vessel* comes from medieval times when alchemy was popular. The vessel is the container, a feminine image where the alchemist worked, not literally to transform lead into gold, but to work toward spiritual transformation, to become whole. "Mary is the vessel for the gestation of the divine incarnated as Jesus, and then for all of us." Furthermore, this vessel contains light and dark, the opposites. That is, each image has a negative side, too, which we need to be conscious of if we are to be spiritually mature. The dark side of *Vessel* is a "captivity that inhibits us"; the dark side of joy, to "believe it will last forever." We must let go of ego self-centeredness in order to be transformed. Becoming more mature spiritually, we penetrate more deeply into soul experience "so that the gold of God-centered wholeness can appear." Each reflection is followed by a prayer that helps to center us in Mary's presence, experiencing the depth of our own self/Self. The value of such an approach emphasizes that religious images and doctrines are related to us personally, that we, too, carry the "gold."

The author feels that the first depth psychologists were the mystics. C. G. Jung wrote of the thirteenth-century German mystic and teacher Meister Eckhart that he had gone deeper than the archetypal level into the great mystery of God. As Richo notes, we are in the realm of imagination here; the realm of the feminine. "Imagination," he writes, "is the nature and activity of the soul, the point of meeting between the ego and the Self." And again, "To let our imagination be moved by the titles of Mary is a form of prayer to her, since full release of imagination requires a surrender." Years ago, Thomas Merton wrote that the crisis of our age is a "widespread poverty, even more, a *captivity*, of imagination." And of religious metaphor, Merton wrote, "We have become suspicious of that for which we are starved." In this book, we are given nourishing food for the journey toward becoming more spiritually mature persons, enabling us to be more fully Christ and Mary in the world.

Focusing on grace and prayer as motifs throughout, Richo writes, "Grace is the free gift of spiritual energy and momentum that complements us and shows us the divine potential in ourselves." It is grace that liberates, gives life, and transforms. For Jung, the soul "speaks" whether in personal dreams or in age old religious images that carry spiritual energy. Praying with the images in the Litany of Loreto can draw us inward to depths of soul where we experience a flash like Wordsworth's "flash that has revealed (or reveals) the invisible world."

In the appendix "A Retreat with Mary," the author encourages prayer with suggestions for various ways of praying with music, art, movement, silence, and so on, as well as being with the image, and asking, "What is the felt sense in you stirred by the title?" Becoming conscious of a "flash of Divinity within," we may sense more fully our unity with the ever present divine feminine, with each other, with nature, and the cosmos.

When Mary Becomes Cosmic is overdue for those longing for more self-insight. I feel that you, the reader, will return to this book often to savor its wisdom and treasure the gift of the cosmic Mary.

—Mariann Burke, RSCJ

Introduction

*[Mary] advanced in her pilgrimage of faith
and at the same time, in a discreet, yet direct
and effective way, she made present to
humanity the mystery of Christ and
she still continues to do so.*

—Pope St. John Paul II,
Redemptoris Mater, 1987

It is a touching fact that Mary is the most loved woman on earth. A powerful and loving mother who is loved and loves us all is not an invention of Catholicism. The divine feminine expressed as *the Great Mother* has an ancient history in the collective psyche of humankind. Only her names have changed over the centuries while her support of humanity remains the same. In the Christian tradition, we can say that since medieval times, praying to Mary has been constant. It is as if the whole planet were one uninterrupted and joyously trusting chant to the Great Mother, the divine feminine in God.

In an Angelus Address in 1978, Pope John Paul I said, "God is Father and even more God is Mother." The divine feminine refers to qualities in the Godhead that are traditionally associated with the feminine. This includes relatedness, nurturance, protectiveness, and openness. Likewise, the divine feminine focuses strongly on the power of *grace* in spirituality rather than spiritual practices only. Popular piety often preserves the profound wisdom of the psyche—no matter what official teaching sources say.

In the archetypally meaningful story of St. Catherine Laboure's vision of Mary, she saw the Madonna wearing rings on every finger. Some emitted rays of light that extended into the world. Some gave no light at all. When St. Catherine asked about this, Mary said, "The rays of light are the graces I give to those who ask; the rings with no light hold the graces no one has asked me for yet." We have not begun to ask what Mary can give. We have thus not dared to let ourselves believe in her fully. We have yet to imagine how committed she is to us as mother and advocate. Thomas Merton wrote in a poem, "Where in the world has any voice / Prayed to you, Lady, for the peace that's in your power?"[1]

Masculine energy is associated with finding solutions to problems especially through effort and logic. Yet there is a steady and enduring trust in the divine feminine as even more helpful in finding solutions to our personal and political problems through grace and faith. Here is an example: While he was a student in Germany, Pope Francis was touched by an image of "Mary, the Untier of Knots," a title that reminds us of the overlooked assistance we can find in the feminine, if only our level of trust could expand.

Catholics over the centuries have preserved consciousness of and devotion to Mary. When we title Mary *Mother of All the Living*, it is important to realize that we mean just that. Her care does not extend only to Catholics; it is equally bestowed on all humans everywhere, without exception, irrespective of creed or condition. We see the bigness of Mary in the history of our world when we no longer restrict her miracles for Catholics only but for everyone. Likewise, the title *Mother of All the Living* refers to all beings and the whole cosmos. The extent of the divine feminine caretaking is boundless.

The chapters that follow draw from many religious traditions. This is in keeping with the encouragement of the Second Vatican Council: "We acknowledge, preserve, and promote the spiritual and moral goods found in other religious traditions." The word *catholic* means "universal." A universal Catholic is one who is open to truths from all sources. Such openness is a virtue that leads to the discovery of corresponding truths immemorially preserved in all spiritual traditions and ultimately within ourselves.

Our psyche indeed contains the whole heritage of our collective humanity. The Great Mother meets us in such universality. This will be a central theme in the chapters that follow. *There is a cosmic Christ; there is a cosmic Mary; there is a cosmic Self in every one of us.* Cosmic, in this context, refers to the bigness of our faith when it includes the entire universe in its embrace. We move from focusing only on our own salvation to a deep caring about all creation. We see a reference to this bigness in the Gospel of John: "God so loved the *world...*" (3:16, emphasis added).

The sweet images of Mary, without earthiness or passion, depict a broken, restricted, and abridged archetype of the divine feminine. The Madonna most of us grew up with was all about comfort, and she does indeed offer that in a nonstop way. But she is also the challenger, the one who calls us to join her in her unceasing battle for justice, to care with activist compassion for the downtrodden. She wants to bring us to the smelly, excluded, disenfranchised, marginalized members of our society because that is where she is. Cardinal Walter Kasper at the Mary and the Unity of the Church Ecumenical Conference in 2008 wrote, "Mary does not stand for the mighty, the haughty and the rich; she stands for the little ones, the powerless, the poor, the meek, the humble. She is tender with the sick and the disabled, tender also with the sinners."

There is the image of Mary from Central America showing her with dark skin under the title *Madre de los Desaparecidos* (Mother of the Disappeared). Mary is representing the mothers of those who were kidnapped and killed. Mary is the archetype of help before, during, and after the injustices. Our challenge is to ask for more and more from Mary, Protectress of the Helpless. This allows the archetype of divine feminine to evolve more fully in our consciousness. She was always complete, but each century reveals more of who she is and can be for us.

Thus, Mary is the champion, the fierce tigress for justice. This is the opposite of the unattainable, remote Madonna in traditional iconography. Those images "keep her in her place" rather than acknowledge that her place is everywhere: she is one of us and for the least of us. This Mary does not support a privileged white ego. She is best pictured as the black Madonna, the creatively erotic earth mother who keeps her promise to guide and protect our planet. Our title for her has to be like Shakespeare's reference to Juliet: "the hopeful lady of my earth."

We see in Mary the importance of our own calling to bring a prophetic vision to the world. We practice reaching this imaginative vision through a combination of contemplation and focus on world problems with an apostolic intent. Prophetic imagination means trusting divine power in history and envisioning more of it in the future. The apostolic intent is how we join in that venture with God by our work and mission. Jesus is our model and it is he who gives us the graces to do this.

My concern is that many Catholics seem to reduce their devotion to Mary as they mature in age and in understanding. Unfortunately, Mary often does not survive our growing up, and that is unfortunate since she carries an ingredient so essential to our spiritual development, the powers of the feminine. Mary has to survive today in a whole new way. Less devotion to Mary nowadays is not about more devotion to Jesus; it is about less consciousness of the role of the feminine in the story of our salvation. Paradoxically, once we acknowledge the divine feminine, we find Jesus more fully. This is because he represents wholeness; what we mean when we say he is divine.

Is there a way to come back to the center, to let go of sentimental piety and yet honor Mary fervently? Can such mature devotion and consciousness of Mary help us open to more respect for women? There is a direct connection between who Mary is and what all women are in their full empowerment. This book presents a way to renew our devotion grounded in the depth of such psychic truth, one and the same as faith truth.

The first challenge is to make our devotion to Mary and our understanding of her more adult. This book offers some paths—through text, contemplation, and prayers—to that maturity: visioning her not only as the Mary of faith, but also as an archetypal energy that endures in the universe, acknowledging her dark side with all its fertile potential, freeing ourselves from any disabling literalism in our appreciation of her, becoming aware of her cosmic dimensions.

The result is a love of Mary that stands up to our own personal evolution and the advances of science.

The new vision of her is simultaneously a self-discovery. She is no longer the Madonna out there but the mother, virgin, and wise guide in our interior life and, in that of the universe, a divine mirror of human and natural reality in its most exultant state. In the Hebrew Bible, Judith disarmed Holofernes—symbolic of the male ego—with the beauty of her face. All our lives, we have seen Mary pictured as a beautiful woman. Her beauty is not meant to represent remoteness. It is symbolic of the divine wholeness in all of us. An object of devotion is beautiful precisely in order that we be drawn to it as a mirror of what we are called to be, whole and wholly devoted to a life of caring love. Likewise, beauty is connected not to timid submissiveness, but to strength as in the example of Judith.

I was in Rome during the writing of this book, when the Pilgrim Madonna came to St. Peter's Basilica. This is a statue of Our Lady of Fatima that travels from country to country as a pilgrim of peace. My sense of devotion led me to join the thousands of devotees who had come to honor her. As I passed in front of the statue of the Madonna banked with flowers and candles, I remember thinking how small the statue was compared to what I expected. I felt there was something so touching about the smallness. It proclaimed humility in the midst of the vast grandeur of the basilica. The image looked so utterly serene and yet so powerfully present. I felt Mary's presence in that moment more really than ever. The crowds were so large that we could only pass by the statue, not stop to contemplate it. After passing it, I turned to look back at it to get one more glimpse. Suddenly, in the midst of my intense and prayerful gazing at the Madonna, I heard a voice speaking so clearly inside me: "Imagine, *that presence* is what is inside each of us, something that beautiful, powerful, and perfect." It was the very point of this book! In effect, the statue had become, in that moment, a vision of Mary, and I was hearing her speak to me. It was not a voice of my mind's making. It was the immortal feminine revealing itself in mortal words. St. Peter's Basilica was such an apt—and ironic—place for that connection to happen.

It is significant, too, that my revelation came while walking away from—that is letting go of—the experience. This recalls an archetypal story. In the *Aeneid*, the hero Aeneas is visited by a messenger/huntress in the woods. Only as they are parting does he recognize in her the effulgent splendor of his heavenly mother, Venus, who was known as *Mother of Rome*. We see this same realization also in the poem by Emily Dickinson that begins, "By a departing light / We see acuter, quite."[2]

After returning home, I told my breathtaking story to a mentor and friend, Sidney Lanier, a retired Anglican priest and a descendent of poets. He said without hesitation—again I was hearing something not conjured by my mind—that the event I described was a completion of my priestly ordination. He said that I had been ordained a priest in the Word (Logos) originally, but now was ordained anew in Wisdom (Sophia) right there in St. Peter's Basilica. He added, "The spiritual feminine in you was suddenly mirrored by the spiritual feminine represented in the statue."

Perhaps all visions are just such realizations of how the transcendent mirrors and reveals our psychic depths and those of the cosmos. We finally come to see that separateness is illusory, that the infinite is in the finite, not above it. Mary does not appear to people to bring heaven *to* our hearts but to expose the heaven *within* our hearts. And all that remains for us is to release our exuberant gratitude.

Most of what you are about to read was written with a special and unusual intuition I did not have when I sat down to write. In my writing of these pages, Mary continually instilled new perspectives, opened new vistas, adorned my imagination, and surprised me with a knowledge I know I did not have before. It is what she wanted me to know, and I pass it on to you. There will never be poetry fluent enough to praise her, and there will barely be time to fulfill her only request, that we love the world as she does.

> My knowledge is so weak, O blissful Queen,
> To tell abroad thy mighty worthiness...
> Guide thou my song.
>
> —Geoffrey Chaucer,
> "The Prioress's Tale," *Canterbury Tales*

CHAPTER ONE

Who Is Mary?

She is a muscle of love, this Mary. I feel her in unexpected moments, her Assumption into heaven happening in places inside me. She suddenly rises, and when she does, she does not go up, up into the sky, but further and further inside me....She goes into all the holes life has gouged out of us.

—Sue Monk Kidd, *The Secret Life of Bees*

This book is a Jungian contemplation of Mary as an archetype of the divine feminine. It is mythic-psychological. It is not meant to be a treatise on theology, though I often include theological references to show their correlation with the archetypal view.

Theology looks at biblical and Church teachings in order to present them in contemporary ways. Its purpose is ultimately to appreciate divine love and show how it can act in us. Jungian psychology is a branch of depth psychology. Along with its focus on clinical practice, it looks at perennial themes in all religions to see how they reflect the hidden contents of the human psyche. Its purpose is to show us ways to access our inner wholeness. Both theology and depth psychology reflect the divine and human dimensions of life. There is no contradiction between them; indeed, they complement each other.

This book presents a contemplative form of depth psychology. It attempts to show how religious teachings tell us about our deepest selves, specifically about the divine feminine in all of us and in the cosmos.

We can focus on three ways of looking at Mary: the historical person who now is the object of faith, the universal archetype she represents, and the object of our personal devotion. In the chapters that follow, we will see how they are intricately connected.

The first way—Mary as the historical person—presents her as the actual woman who lived in Nazareth, one of us, a human person. We know hardly anything about her daily life. The historical Mary, like the historical Jesus, is not clearly accessible in the New Testament, which is not a news report but a faith document written from faith to faith. In the New Testament, we see this Mary as the Mother of Jesus, his first disciple, the one who encourages his first miracle, who stands by his cross, and who receives his Holy Spirit at Pentecost.

The Church reflected on the Mary of faith and came to see her as ever-blessed, as free from sin from the first moment of her life, as raised to heaven at the last moment of her life, as interceding for all of us during all our life. This Mary, born in time and now sharing Christ's risen life, is the subject of magisterial doctrine and theological discussion. The theology of Mary, Mariology, is rooted in Christology, focusing on the mysteries of the incarnation and redemption. Much of Mariology is based on the teachings of the early Church fathers that presented Mary as the new Eve who says yes rather than no to God's plan. Likewise, Church teaching is based not only on Scripture but on Tradition that includes patristics, the evolving history of doctrine, liturgy, mystical revelations, and the ongoing faith of believers, known as the *sensus fidelium*. Tradition also includes an attention to apparitions of Mary showing her ongoing care for humanity. Examples are the Madonna of Guadalupe seen by St. Juan Diego and the Madonna of Lourdes seen by St. Bernadette. The sources of Tradition constantly validate the legitimacy of veneration of Mary.

Thus, the first presentation of Mary combines history, the gospel, and theology.

A second way of considering Mary is as the holder of the archetype of the divine feminine, an age-old expression of the wholeness of God. She is venerated as a *source* of blessings and addressed in that way. This differs from veneration of the Mary of theology who is addressed as a *mediator* with Christ. Thus, the "theologically correct" prayer to Mary is "Pray to Christ for us." In other words, we are asking her to intercede on our behalf. Many of us, however, have indeed addressed petitions to Mary directly. We have shared our sorrows and challenges with her. We have asked her assistance and accompaniment. When we did that, we were venerating the divine feminine.

An archetype, as we shall see, is a motif, a familiar theme in stories and dreams. It is also an instinctive psychic energy within our own spiritual and bodily consciousness. Archetypes appear in persons, dream figures, story characters, and numinous events. This second way of understanding Mary is the province of depth psychology found in this book. The archetypal Mary is larger than her personal history, so she is portrayed as a spiritual energy in us and in the entire cosmos. We see this archetypal perspective in the writings of the mystics, who were, in my view, the first depth and transpersonal psychologists. The archetypal Great Mother is the divine feminine, not the Mary of Catholic theology. In the chapters that follow, we will benefit from exploring their common characteristics in theology and depth psychology.

The third Mary is the familiar object of a devotion that has its origins in the early Church. The purpose of a healthy devotion is to foster a personal relationship with God and the saints, especially Mary. A quality of an archetype is that, when it manifests, strong feelings arise in the beholder. When a devotee is ardent, we see how the Mary of faith and the divine feminine archetype are linked *through* devotion.

There is an ancient and ineradicable inclination in the human psyche to honor the divine feminine, the Great Mother. Our inclination to venerate the divine feminine explains, in part, the durability of popular piety toward Mary over these centuries.

We can, however, design a healthy devotion to Mary— one based on the theology of the Second Vatican Council and the liturgy along with an appreciation of archetypal meanings. Such devotion then makes Mary present in our own immediate experience in powerful and empowering ways. Devotion is directed both to the Mary of faith and to the archetypal feminine. Devotion is a crucial and essential component of religion and depth psychology. Carl Jung showed us how the power of images activate, encourage, and challenge our higher Self. We access biblical images of Mary listed in the Litany of Loreto as a pathway into the richness of the divine feminine as presented in Jungian and mystical perspectives. Thus, all three aspects of the Madonna come together into one: Mary of faith, archetype of the divine feminine, and object of devotion.

Recently, I viewed a Japanese interpretation of the Madonna. It occurred to me that, although Mary herself certainly did not look Japanese, the image was still quite appropriate. The image portrays the divine feminine whereby women of any culture and nationality can be depicted as Mary. In fact, the original Mary of history and of devotion is now much bigger than her story or her physical appearance.

ARCHETYPES AS SPIRITUAL ENERGIES

I myself must be the Virgin and bring forth God from within me if I am to be given the grace of divine joy.
—Angelus Silesius, "The Spiritual Virgin"

According to Jungian psychology, there is both a masculine and a feminine energy in the psyche of all humans and in all of nature. Masculine and feminine in this context are not equated with male or female nor are they limited to males or females. They are psyche-energies, qualities in all of us inherited from our human ancestry. The term *divine feminine* in this book is not reserved to females. It is a quality of all beings and of God in whose image they are made.

Archetypes are energies expressed in characters and themes that keep appearing in the lives and minds of all humans. They have done so from ancient times. Archetypes are not merely literary themes but spiritual drives—the same in all of us. Archetypes are thus universal, cross-cultural, transhistorical, and transreligious.

The archetypes are personified as characters in stories the world over. Actually, archetypes articulate the full tapestry of energies in our own life experience and choices: the energy to live through pain as a *hero*, to find wisdom like a *guide*, to pursue a dark purpose as a *shadow*, to protect in a *mother*ly or *father*ly way, to act as the *trickster* who trips up the arrogant ego and gives it its comeuppance. It is the nature of archetypes that every archetypal character—every archetypal energy—is in us.

For Jung, the Self is the central archetype, God's divine life in us and in nature. The Self is like the Atman in Hinduism, our basic goodness in Buddhism, Tao in Taoism, the Beloved in Sufism, and the indwelling of the Holy Spirit in Christianity. In this book, the word *Self* with a capital *S* represents the divine life in us, the life of grace that animates us to live as Christ in the world.

Thus the *Self* will refer also to our inner wholeness, both a reality about us and a call to us to incarnate that divine life in here-and-now reality. Our ego, "I," our self with a small *s*, awaits that embodiment of the divine Self, what Jung called the "ego-Self axis." This is also a mystical realization as we see in *New Seeds of Contemplation* by Thomas Merton: "There is an irreducible opposition between the deep transcendent self that awakens only in contemplation, and the superficial, external self which we commonly identify with the first person singular. Our reality, our true self, is hidden in what appears to us to be nothingness....We can rise above this unreality and recover our hidden reality....God Himself begins to live in me not only as my Creator but as my other and true self."

The challenge of archetypes is thus to hold energies in us and to send out from us the powers that come from them. This is a way we help the planet evolve. For instance, we are each naturally geared to cooperate in order to survive. This is the archetype of the Self as helpful companion.

We can apply this example to our spiritual practice since Christ is the helpful companion always with us and helping us. The life of Christ shows us our calling. We are here to join in Christ's friendliness toward humanity, the purpose of our ongoing spiritual journey. This will not seem alien. It is like aligning ourselves with the energy already and always inside us. Christ's grace does the rest. *We were born to display in our individual life story the divine design that is always in us. This is why we were given a lifetime.*

Our essential Self, in the Jungian view, is our intrinsic nature. It is not conditioned by our human past nor is it constrained by our unique individual story. The Self is the archetype of God in us as unconditional love, perennial wisdom, and healing power. These divine qualities are embodied in our very being: The love is in our hearts; the wisdom is in our minds; and the healing is in our souls. We are not complete as humans until we activate—individuate—these gifts. This is how they represent our calling. There is an innate inclination in us to let this calling be fulfilled in us and through us. That innate inclination is another way of describing an archetype. Archetypes are the equivalent of instincts because they are like drives or inclinations that influence our actions or feelings. For example, we each have a helper energy within us that presents itself when we see others in pain.

All the archetypes are both male and female, but some are primarily associated with male energy—the king, the father, the warrior. Some are primarily associated with female energy—virgin, mother, queen, wise older woman—as we saw above. These are the four specific themes that keep appearing in our images of and prayers to Mary: she shows pure open heartedness to the Divine, expressed as virginity; she is the mother who nurtures us as she nurtured

Jesus; she is Queen-protectress of Heaven and Earth; and she is Sophia who shares her wisdom for the betterment of humanity. These archetypes of openness, nurturance, power, and wisdom are all for the benefit of the world. Likewise, they are archetypes, so they exist in everyone. This is how humanity can benefit from our having been here. Devotion to Mary can help that happen. A personal relationship, fostered by devotion, is the link between the divine life and our human embodiment of it.

Thus, when we love, honor, and invoke Mary, we are preserving the mysterious and significant truths we see in her: We are open to what is unfolding and to what God asks of us. We nurture one another. We use our powers for the good of humanity. We have access to and can share our inner wisdom. Mary is therefore not only an icon above us but also a mirror of our deepest reality. The powers of Mary are the feminine powers in our souls. Her titles are our own names as they are spelled in the language of our cosmic destiny. Mary as the divine feminine is not far away or up above, but in here, in us, and in all that is.

In the Jungian perspective, Mary as an archetype can be viewed as the most recent personification of the great goddess, with names like Demeter, Tara, Isis, Astarte, Inanna, Cybele, Kali, and others. In the archetypal view, therefore, the accent is not on Mary as a person but as a mysterious presence both in the world and as a living component of the human psyche. This is not a new perspective. It seems that no mature religious consciousness in human history has ever been literal in its understanding of stories or persons in their Scriptures, but rather has venerated them for the cosmic and interior truths they embody. For instance, in the eighth century, St. Andrew of Crete wrote, "Mary is a statue sculpted by God as an image of a divine archetype."

One of our tasks in growing to psychological adulthood is to separate from our mother's home and move out on our own. We have to leave the literal mother, but the mother archetype cannot be abandoned, outgrown, or left. It is intrapsychic. It is in us as a component of our human identity. Mary serves as the lifelong prototype of the mother who remains intact all through life, ever with us. This is why she is so crucial in the story of our unfolding destiny and of our very identity.

We now begin to appreciate how our beliefs about God, Christ, Mary, and the saints reflect age-old archetypal meanings. This acknowledgment expands our appreciation both of our faith and ourselves. Maintaining our faith is how we have cherished the Divine in the depths of our human psyche and in the natural world. Commitment to faith is how we live out our calling. We could only have realized this now as the human potential movement is giving way to the divine potential movement. *The Mary of faith and the archetypal Mary continually come together to give us a holistic view of her.*

We can now appreciate how the object of veneration can be an archetypal energy. For example, we honor the archetype of queenship, the energy of feminine power. (An energy is feminine; a person is a female.) A mortal person, an actual female on a throne, is not what people bow to. She is the holder, the representative of queenly energy that has power to represent and protect us. We look at a queen, but we reverence *queenship.* So, for instance, the honor shown to Queen Elizabeth I is the same honor shown to her present successor. The archetype is the same. The individuals are different but each held or holds the same meaning to the people of England. That meaning is in the office the queen represents. The physical queen provides a focus for a deeper significance we are in the presence of. Likewise, Mary of Nazareth, to people of faith, is the holder of the archetype of queenship, which in this instance, is heavenly. It is not that the person who is the holder of the office is not important or worthy of honor. It is that the true object of our reverential regard is a deep archetypal reality in the universe and in all of us. This is why bowing to a statue of Buddha is not aimed at Siddhartha of the fifth century but at the enlightened mind in ourselves and in all beings. He is the most recent holder, representative, and personification of that energy.

WHAT WE ARE BY GRACE

We are saved not by our modest merits and efforts, not by our more or less decent moral behavior or our human deeds, but only by grace.
—Cardinal Walter Kasper, Mary and the Unity of the Church Ecumenical Conference, 2008

The historical Mary is honored as an embodiment of the feminine aspect of God. Mary is by grace what we can be by the same grace, here and now articulations of divine feminine powers that live within our psyche. This is how we see the archetypal Mary as an intrapsychic reality, the energy in us that also reaches out from us so that we can make her love visible. We incarnate her meaning and presence in the world.

How does the incarnational process happen? How does our body, mind-limited humanity embody its cosmic-wide divinity? Mary is the model of how it happens by a combination of surrender and choice. We offer an unconditional yes to grace, surrender, and make a commitment and choice to live it in such a way that all the world can benefit. Thus, our personal experience of a calling and the grace to fulfill it become universal in scope. We are here not only to be personally "saved" but to save the world. Our care for ourselves becomes our caring for the world.

At the incarnation, Christ enters an evolving world. He is the center of evolution because only his story and mystery accommodate the full archetypal picture of humanity—both its story and its potential. Indeed, the life of Christ is the life story of all of us. The epiphany, at which Mary presents Jesus to the Magi, is the symbolic representation of this cosmic destiny. When we show love, wisdom, and healing in the world, we do what Mary did: we present God to all humankind without exception. Our personal completion as humans is the universal calling to share our gifts with the world. Jesus was anointed Messiah to usher in a new way of living, one that values justice, peace, and love. This is the spiritual implication and challenge in the realization that divine figures are archetypes of the powers inside us. Thus, the commands of Christ are his way of giving us portraits of the life we are called to express. All Christ asks is that we be who we really are.

Though we do not know anything clearly about the historical Mary, we intimately know the transhistorical Mary because her reality is in our very souls. The Mary of Nazareth is not irrelevant, however. She is the physical foundation of the archetype of the divine feminine. There was probably an actual heroic or wonder-working woman in the origins of beliefs in all the mythic goddesses. Ariadne of the labyrinth and Queen Arete, mother of Nausicaa, in Homer's *Odyssey* are described as mortal females who were honored as personifications of the great goddess. It is significant that Ariadne is a virgin and Arete is a mother and a queen. They too thus represent the ever-common theme of the three component qualities of the goddess.

The theological issue, however, is not whether the historical Mary is important but *how* she is important. She is the personal vehicle by which the transpersonal mother-energy enters our era. The historical Mary's willingness to say yes to the divine design makes her the fitting instrument for an archetypal purpose. The historical Mary is still to be honored while always remembering that she is a means not an end, a means to make contact with a mystery that cannot be contained—only approximately described —in human metaphors.[1]

We can reinterpret traditional teachings in the light of contemporary needs and scientific/psychological advances. Such theologizing is found more and more in depth psychology.

A distinction may help us understand some of this. Some things hold in principle, for example, a law. However, a *de facto* law, that is, "as it is in practice or in reality," may be viewed with great latitude. As a theological principle, Mary, virgin mother of God, is a human being, endowed by God with privileges, who now intercedes for us. *De facto*, Mary in Mediterranean countries, eastern European, and in Central and South America has gathered archetypal meanings. Thus, she is treated as more than a person *de facto* in earthy piety. This is not idolatry, only recognition of the divine feminine that has ineluctably survived—though it is not theologically sound in an official sense, it is, in principle.

Nonetheless, Mary is not a *goddess*, which is too limited a term for her archetypal significance. The word *goddess* may turn us off because it has a hoary, pagan, and new-age ring to it. On the other hand, it stands as a metaphor for the divine feminine.

Religious metaphors are not simply literary devices. They are confirmations of a spiritual truth unexplainable by logic. They point to a mystery that is larger and vaster than any of our human words or images can contain or describe. A metaphor in literature is an implied comparison. It shows the similarity between two things. A spiritual metaphor goes beyond that and presents a new, unnoticed deeper reality that arises from the two. Such is the sense in which the word *metaphor* is used in this book.

Regarding depth psychology, the dogmas of recent times regarding Mary can be plumbed for their archetypal meaning. Tradition preserves a truth we have only recently allowed ourselves to believe, that the mystery of the divine life is about the depth of our life and that of the cosmos, both replete with longings we were born to fulfill. According to depth psychology, doctrines are callings to us to live out that precious destiny. The doctrines are code names for our own profound identity and spiritual potentials.

The tenacity with which for millennia of Western history both men and women have, in the figure of the Virgin Mary, clung to the veneration of a compassionate and merciful mother attests to the human hunger for such a reassuring image....This tenacity only becomes comprehensible in the context of what we now know about the millennia-long tradition of Goddess worship in prehistory.

—Riane Eisler, *The Chalice and the Blade*

CHAPTER TWO

What Is the Divine Feminine?

The one-sided patriarchal value-canon of western consciousness and the fundamental ignorance regarding the essentially different female and feminine psychology have contributed in a major way to the crisis of our time. Hence, understanding the Feminine is an urgent necessity not only in order to understand the single individual but also to heal the collective.

—Erich Neumann, Lecture for Eranos Conference, 1952

The Council of Ephesus in 431 taught about Christ's divine-human nature and declared Mary to be the Mother of God. Ephesus was sacred to the goddess Diana, and the site of her temple was considered holy ground to the people there. There had been an association with the feminine divinity on that spot from ancient times, predating Diana, the then most recent personification of the universal goddess. A shrine was built to Mary on the same site.

Many pagan temples to goddesses became churches dedicated to Mary. For instance, on Monte Vergine in Italy, there stood a temple to Cybele, the Phrygian (Turkish) "Great Mother, the mother of the gods, the savior who hears our prayers, the always accessible mother." Cybele is the consort of Attis, the dying and rising god whose resurrection was celebrated each spring. In 1119, a church was built at the temple site in honor of Mary. The temple of Cybele in Rome became the site of the basilica of St. Mary Major. Christians easily transferred their allegiance to the goddess onto Mary. No one taught Christians to do any of this. There is in all of us a grassroots, collective natural acknowledgment of the feminine as a necessary and inextricable dimension of the Divine.

Early people possessed what we have lost: an infallible awareness of a generative, sustaining, transfiguring power in the unconscious and in nature. That is the feminine power that oversees and can guide our journey through life. We recall the final words in *Faust* by Goethe: "The eternal feminine draws us onward" ("Das Ewig-Weibliche/Zieht uns hinan").[1]

IN DARKNESS AND IN LIGHT

The Great Mother remains true to her essential, eternal, and mysterious darkness, in which she is the center of the mystery of existence.

—Erich Neumann

As can be seen, archetypal energies have a light and a dark side. This follows from the fact that they represent wholeness. In Christian tradition, St. Clement of Rome taught that God rules the world with his right hand in the form of Christ and with his left hand in the form of Satan. This view combines apparent opposites as complementaries rather than maintaining a dualistic view of the celestial and the demonic.

Recently, Mary Magdalene has become an archetype for New Age spirituality. She represents the passionate side of the feminine. Our idealized images of who Mary is lack a shadow element—mysterious, earthy, not evil—to be wholly expressive of the divine feminine. Otherwise, she is not whole. The exalted image of Mary emerges from a masculine stereotype of the nurturant feminine; it avoids and cancels the wild destructive feminine, the dark side, so visible in mother nature. She is the goddess of conception but of putrefaction too. This is how she is midwife to resurrection.

The shadow of the Divine comes through in the fact that initiation—a prerequisite of our spiritual evolution—is painful. This is because the shadow of the divine feminine is the nemesis of the arrogant inflated ego. The purpose of this shadow side is to grant hegemony to the higher Self, to depose the fearful ego in favor of uninhibited love, to free the ignorant ego so it can find wisdom, to break the clench of pride so a healthy humility can appear. This dismantling of the ego will feel like annihilation but it is actually a helpful comeuppance, a path to liberation. In *The Heart of Matter*, Pierre Teilhard de Chardin suggests that we should welcome the comeuppance: "My God, I deliver myself up with utter abandon to those fearful forces of dissolution which, I blindly believe, will this day cause my narrow ego to be replaced by your divine presence."[2]

The dark side of the feminine is aimed precisely at impressing the ego into the service of the Divine so that it can find its true status of service to people and the planet. All of this has been excluded from our sense of who Mary is. As our faith becomes big enough to hold the full feminine archetype—light and dark—we will appreciate the wholeness of Mary, both comforter and challenger.

All the ancient images of the destructive side of the goddess include the theme of regeneration. The symbol of the vulture is an example. She hovers over death, but she then transforms it into her own living tissue and food for her young. The dark side of the feminine is found in its transformative function, which necessarily involves destruction. The conditions of existence in nature include pain, death, storms, and stress as legitimate features of planetary evolution. Yet regeneration always follows. The destructive conditions of nature are thus friendly in the unfolding of our evolutionary story.

In pre-Christian times, the initiatory rites of regeneration were celebrated at Eleusis in Greece in honor of the mother goddess Demeter. Cicero wrote of Eleusis, "We have been given a reason not only to live in joy but to die with better hope." The torch-lit procession there each night was like the one that now takes place at Lourdes.

When I myself went to Eleusis, I visited a chapel in honor of Mary on the hill above the ancient pagan shrine. Early Christians believed she was carried there by angels so she, too, could be initiated in preparation for the annunciation. The mythical story is a touching way of showing how certain the psyche is that the mother energy is associated with initiation. In fact, after the shrine of Eleusis was closed in Christian times, people would say as they passed by it, "Forsaken Eleusis celebrates herself." The earth energy of dying and rising is indestructible and outlives the forms of religion and the vagaries of human attention. Mother nature continues the ritual of death and resurrection with or without our participation. The dark side, the shadow, is thus nothing to fear; it is our passport to a richer life.

There are two ways of considering the shadow: the shadow of the human will can be *evil*; the shadow of natural reality is simply *corrective*. Arson is an example of a human choice that arises from evil intent. A forest fire by spontaneous combustion is a dark event but also a gift of nature that ultimately helps trees flourish. It is not an evil choice meant to inflict pain but a necessary condition for growth. It is the dissolving power within nature that grants an opportunity to evolve. Corrective evil is dark for the sake of light; willed evil is dark for the sake of dark.

Mary was presented to us as our prompt and perpetual help, and we love the consolations of her presence. Yet we seem unable to meet her as the terrifying mother who helps us grow through pain. Terrifying means frightening to the ego that cannot believe there is grace behind the terror. To invoke Mary for an exemption from the conditions of existence is to invoke her against herself. Initiatory pain is her necessary dark side. This is precisely how she helps us.

The way of the cross is an example of how a necessary darkness is a path to resurrection. This does not refer only to the darkness of personal or physical suffering in the course of life. Once we embrace the mystery of the cross, we accept that the world may show contempt for us—even harm or kill us. Our commitment to be Christ in the world means that we can expect no better treatment than his. But we trust that evil, though real, does not have the last word.

When Mary stays at the cross, she is the sentinel of our spiritual purpose to face evil nonviolently. The image of the women at the foot of the cross is a way of affirming the role of the feminine in initiating our egos into that costly but courageously redemptive calling. Christ redeeming us did not mean that he was a victim *of* pain but a victor *through* pain. From the archetypal perspective, all this was instinctively known in the spiritual psyche and so it finds its way into the gospel story. Inspiration of the evangelists is precisely this reliable evocation of the inner archetypal voice of collective wisdom.

Prayer to the dark side of Mary is thus for strength to bear difficulties not to delete them. We would not be respecting ourselves as creatures of light and dark if we wanted Mary to prevent our having to go on the full journey of life, with all its necessary and implacable givens. The mother (*mater*) archetype represents the essential goodness of matter whether it come as hurricane or breeze. Looking at the *whole* earth, "God saw everything that he had made, and indeed, it was very good" (Gen 1:31).

RESTORING MARY TO HER WHOLENESS

The only way to make life bearable is to love and adore that which, beneath everything, animates and directs it.

—Pierre Teilhard de Chardin,
Letters from a Traveller

Throughout the centuries, we idealized Mary and demonized Eve, thus splitting the female archetype and creating good mother and bad mother images. The challenge for us now is to allow our sense of Mary the full panoply of qualities of an archetype. These include a dark side, a connection to nature, and bodiliness—coincidentally, the attributes a patriarchy finds suspicious or dangerous. For instance, Mary can be seen both as the nuturing mother who comforts us and the ego-devouring mother who transmutes us. She can have more connection to nature. She can be presented with more fully female features. Images of Mary, prayers to her, and theological speculation about her will begin to include the three missing pieces so that she/we can be whole.

Dark Side

In other traditions, the female archetype has unabashedly included the dark side. Apuleius, in *The Golden Ass*, associates Venus, goddess of love, with the dark goddess of the underworld: "Persephone, strike us with the terror of midnight cries." In India, Kali, a mother goddess, has three qualities: goodness, passion, and darkness. She is motherly and erotic. She is destructive of the arrogant ego in ruthless ways that then turn into the kindest of mercies.

The numinous is both fascinating and terrifying. The paradox of the goddess archetype is that it has both fear and love in it. It is the feminine seduction that draws us and the feminine wrath that frightens us. We have been afraid to apply those two to Mary. We have not appreciated her ability to hold both shadow and light. Yet she stands comfortably between them as is commemorated in this line in a poem by Cynewulf: "Hail thou glory of this middle-world!"[3]

To see Mary's wholeness leads to a discovery of the shadow in ourselves. We may fear making Mary complete because it will mean making ourselves complete. It is time to take adult responsibility for our own *disturbing wholeness* rather than to continue dividing the world into angels and demons.

Emma Jung writes in *The Holy Grail*: "An inner wholeness presses its still unfulfilled claims upon us." Something in us yearns for completion, a fascinating and terrifying prospect, requiring the aid of a fully developed divine feminine energy. The "something" is grace, of which Mary is full and fully giving, both to us and in us.

Nature

"It is the whole of nature, extending from the beginning to the end that constitutes the one image of the God Who Is." These words of St. Gregory of Nyssa in "On the Creation of Humanity" demostrate the connection between the Divine and the natural. The feminine association with nature, "mother nature," reminds us that, from earliest times, the earth was thought to be generated by a mother goddess, the creative principle of the universe. We recall the nature titles in the litany to Isis in *The Golden Ass* by Apuleius: "Queen of the Stars, Mother of the Seasons, Mistress of the Universe."

As the world moved from an agrarian, nature-oriented style to a militaristic, aggression-oriented style the patriarchal powers reconfigured myths to suit their purposes and to ensure their authority. For instance, the concept of a Creator God as having no beginning suits the patriarchal denial of the need for a feminine creative principle. We see this also in recent times in the story of Frankenstein, a male doctor who, without the aid of a woman, creates a creature. Joseph Campbell, in his famous television interviews with Bill Moyers, points out that the psyche does not accept such statements in the Bible as "the bosom of Abraham."

In the Judeo-Christian tradition, we already honor things and places that represent fertility, such as a spring, as at Lourdes, or vessels, such as the ark of the covenant. The complete Mary is earth in its heavenward direction.

Black Madonnas may signify this connection with nature. The mother goddess of Egypt, Isis, was black too. The blackness is that of the fertile black earth. The dark also represents the mystery of a reality that is still deeply unconscious. In alchemy, the symbolic process of transformation of the leaden ego into the golden Self begins with *nigredo*, the blackness. Darkness is so often the connection between living archetypal images that come together, as for example, suffering and resurrection.

Mother nature can also be a metaphor for the vast and boundless interiors of the psyche. Wallace Stevens, in *Notes toward a Supreme Fiction*, says, "Perhaps the truth depends upon a walk around the lake."[4] Contact with nature is as useful a way of finding spiritual truths as are logic and intuition. For the psalmist, nature seems to be a *means* of grace: making me "lie down in green pastures...beside still waters" is *how* "he restores my soul" (Ps 23:2–3).

Natural metaphors tell us so much about ourselves. Nature works by alternations of growth and change, of solution and dissolution, like the cycles of our own lifespan and relationships. We can turn to natural images to find comfort in times of confusion: when we find the ever-changing phases of a particular relationship hard to handle, we can meditate on the calm phases of the moon. An irritation in life may remind us to appreciate the pearl-forming oyster. The tree that survives the fire may give us hope when our world goes up in flames. The natural cosmos is a moving affirmation of the psyche and its ever-renewing powers.

Just as the archetype of the divine feminine is within us, so is nature within us as we see in this quotation from *The Lost Gospel of the Earth* by Tom Hayden: "We need to experience nature and the universe as within ourselves, not as external scenery we view outside the window of real life."

Mary as mother is Mary as close to nature. The feminine-nature religious tradition, in medieval times, became associated with witchcraft and was a target of fierce suppression by the patriarchal authorities. Today, we are deeply conscious of the role of nature in bringing us closer to God, of the importance of respect for the planet as a spiritual commitment, and of personal spirituality as ecological awareness. We recall the words of Pope Francis:

> Everything is related, and we human beings are united as brothers and sisters on a wonderful pilgrimage, woven together by the love God has for each of his creatures and which also unites us in fond affection with brother sun, sister moon, brother river and mother earth. (*Laudato Si'* 92)

Bodiliness

Archetypal truths do not stop in the mind but resonate in our bodies. In addition to including the shadow and nature, Mary's image in art and in our hearts is also ready to include bodiliness, human sensuality. Perhaps artists can now bring a respectful sensuousness to pictures of Mary, as we see in images of the Hindu goddesses or in the famous *Madonna* by Edvard Munch. Mary should no longer be the only mother depicted without breasts. Nor does she have to appear as a mother only, as in most pictures of the Holy Family in which she is usually not looking at her spouse, only at her child. She loses her full humanity when she is depicted in the puritanical style that opposes the spiritual to the material world. This is a denial of the incarnation as the way divine consciousness enters time. Mary is an incarnate energy, not a disembodied spirit. The historical Mary is a connection to this dimension of fleshly sensuousness in the feminine archetype, and it can be pictured, imagined, and contemplated this way.

St. Bernard, in his commentaries on The Song of Songs, recommends a practice of imaging ourselves kissing Christ's feet as a sign of repentance, kissing his hands as a request for grace, and yes, kissing his lips as an acknowledgment of union. Mystics, especially St. Teresa of Avila, had no problem speaking of their love for the Divine in even more earthy, sensuous, or sexual terms. We can still retrieve that mystical daring.

> *There are really only two ways, it seems to me, in which we can think about our existence here on earth. We either agree with Macbeth that life is nothing more than a "tale told by an idiot," a purposeless emergence of life-forms including the clever, greedy, selfish, and unfortunate species that we call* Homo sapiens—*the "evolutionary goof." Or we believe that, as Pierre Teilhard de Chardin put it, "There is something afoot in the universe, something that looks like gestation and birth." In other words, a plan, a purpose to it all.*
>
> —Jane Goodall, *Reason for Hope: A Spiritual Journey*

CHAPTER THREE

Powers for Us and in Us

The Tao is the Great Mother, empty and yet overflowing, bringing forth the infinite universe. And it is forever inside you.

—Tao Te Ching

In the next two chapters, we will explore the cosmic energies we find in the titles of Mary listed in the traditional prayer, the Litany of Loreto. A litany is a list of titles of God or of a saint. Each title is a name for an archetypal element of a single spiritual reality. We see this concept in Islam in the "ninety-nine names of God." In the Litany of Loreto, each invocation is followed by a prayer for help.

Litanies to Mary appear in early times in the Church. For instance, in the fourth century, St. Cyril of Alexandria wrote this litany to Mary: "Hail, Mary, Mother of God, Venerable Treasure of the entire Church, Inextinguishable Lamp, Crown of Virginity, Sceptre of True Doctrine, Indissoluble Temple, Abode of Him Who is Infinite, Mother and Virgin." This exuberant praise, reminiscent of goddess ritual prayers, shows that an archetypal Mary was evident and honored even before the Council of Ephesus.

The first written Italian version of the Litany of Loreto is dated 1576. It was recited in Loreto, a small town in Italy where the house of Mary, according to pious tradition, was transported from Nazareth by angels during the Crusades. *Loreto* means "laurel grove," which is where the house first appeared on the Italian landscape. Medieval people made pilgrimages there and brought the Litany home with them. The Jesuit St. Peter Canisius had it printed in 1558 in Dilligen, Germany.

The titles are biblical in origin but each is poetic, imagistic, mystical, and mythic. They are thereby meant to describe and access the feminine dimension of the higher Self in all of us. They do not originate in or make sense to the linear cognitive mind. Cardinal Wiseman is quoted as saying, "The Litany…is not a studied prayer, intended to have logical connection of parts, but is a hymn of admiration and love."[1]

Most of the titles are symbols from the Hebrew Bible that acknowledge the role of the feminine in the mystery of salvation and of wholeness. The titles of the Litany, with our responses, form a profound spiritual guide to and a mysterious mystical code about what wholeness really is. This is the first book that interprets the Litany of Loreto in this way.

We may never have fully accessed or explored the wisdom and nurturing potential of the Litany. We may not have guessed the impact it can have on our lives. Contemplation of the Litany may allow that to happen. This takes meditating on the invocations and fervently praying them. They are sources that become resources when we cultivate them as gardeners cultivate flowers.

The psalmist sings, "As a deer longs for flowing streams, / so my soul longs for you, O God" (Ps 42:1). Deer have a life-sustaining habit that resembles a walking meditation. They pace in a circle where they know there is water, and by treading the same ground over and over, they cause the water to rise to the surface. This is a fertile metaphor for contemplation. A mystery yields up a revelation when we keep contemplating it with no attempt to solve or resolve it. We contemplate the Litany of Loreto again and again, circling it in our hearts. We allow its words and images to reach into us and touch us with no attempt to analyze them. When we do this, a nourishing *wisdom* arises effortlessly for us in three ways: we discover the qualities of the divine feminine; we realize that the titles of Mary describe our inner wholeness; and we find the multiform graces that they promise and provide. We have found our identity as individual articulations of spiritual wholeness.

Such graces are what has accounted for the appeal of the Litany over the centuries. The titles are the realizations of sanctity, and they reflect the deepest truths in our collective being. At that depth, we are one with those who have preceded us and linked to those who will follow us. That continuity is the communion of saints. This is not news but a confirmation of an inner and ancient certainty about the vastness of our human heritage. It is comforting to know that our deepest intuitions are shared by saints, sages, and mystics. Sages, in fact, are simply those who have enunciated aloud the collective wisdom of the ages in striking, poetic, and memorable ways. The full spectrum of spiritual knowledge is indelible in every one of us, often silent or secret. Our psyches are channels of wisdom like nature and like scriptures. Spiritual truths come from the same place in us where there is only one of us. That "place" is the Holy

Spirit. The indwelling Spirit in each of us is a holograph of the entirety of revelation. *Can we trust the Holy Spirit enough to make us believe this?*

The titles of Mary in the Litany of Loreto are, likewise, the many names of our souls, the tongues of pentecostal fire always above our heads. We invoke Mary to arouse and activate those energies in our daily life. In other words, the Litany is a plea for embodiment. It is a blueprint of the feminine archetype in our collective psyche, an outline of our destiny to form and transform the universe. The titles of the Litany create a unique vision of the soul by summoning up feminine qualities.

Similarly, we also see the qualities of the masculine divine in the Litanies of the Sacred Heart and of the Holy Name of Jesus. Mary and Jesus represent the divine feminine and masculine energies in the divine life continuously appearing in human history. Both mirror the divine life in us, the indwelling Spirit.

Why are litanies so important compared to other prayers? They have been used universally from ancient times to describe and praise goddesses and gods. The Roman emperors and the Egyptian pharaohs were considered gods and were honored verbally and in writing with litanies. The titles generated images in the minds of the devotees. Such images of the gods and goddesses were at the same time images of their own archetypal life. Thus, litany titles are fields of energy. They describe what is in us potentially and what we are called to display in and distribute to the world. At the same time, each is an empowerment to do so. For instance, the title of Mary *Comfort of the Troubled* is a field of energy we can make present in our troubled world. This is how each title is a calling. When we comfort others, we become the vehicle for divine comfort to reach those who are troubled. This is how the incarnate divine life of Christ works through us in the current world.

We *are* the real presence of the divine feminine when we live out its qualities: mother/nurturant and corrective; virgin/integral and open; queen/powerful and wise. The mother archetype indicates our inclination to create and nurture; the virgin, to serve and contemplate; and the queen, to exercise power for the protection of all beings. This threefold form of the ancient goddess as the young maiden, the mother, and the mature wise woman ruler is reflected richly in the Litany of Loreto. Mary is honored with specific sets of titles referring to her as virgin, mother, and queen. This replication of the ancient past is not a coincidence but another example of how an inner infallible sense in the psyche of humankind contains one and the same wisdom, no matter in which century or in which religious tradition it appears.

In piety, we believe that Mary loves us as a virgin by her pure mindful attention to us, as a mother by her nurturing affection for us, and as a queen by her all-embracing protection of us. Devotion to Mary means opening to these three graces thankfully and sharing them generously. They make our calling bigger than personal salvation; they ready us to be what Mary is now, the servant-guide-protector of the cosmos. We can trust that graces will come to us so that we can find the strength to fulfill our exalted calling. Carl Jung said, "Whoever speaks in primordial images...evokes the beneficent forces in us all."[2]

Our life of prayer can be first a move *toward* the Beloved; then we are *with* the Beloved; finally, we *are* the Beloved. We move from dialogue, twoness, to a oneness in which all divisions are revealed as illusory. All our young lives, we loved Mary as our mother in heaven. We were supplicants who asked for her graces. This corresponds to a movement toward her while she was *above us.* As we matured in faith, we began to see that the mysteries of her life were exemplars of what we were meant to be. We then felt her *beside us.* Finally, we dared to recognize ourselves in her and experienced her energy *within and as our own souls.* We saw that she is the feminine reality of what we are. This is a progression corresponding to the stages of contemplative prayer. We now love her in the core of our souls as the core. *Before, we loved a picture, but now we love the motherly, virginal, royal reality of our own humanness that boasts such a powerful Source within and ever enfolding us.* Mary is indeed the new Eve because she is the new potential of divinity in the cosmos and in all humanity.

Throughout this book, we continually move back and forth from religious to Jungian/mythic perspectives. Now we do this regarding the qualities of the ancient goddess archetype: The mystic philosopher, Pythagoras, reflected that the threefold goddess represented the phases of a woman's life: virgin, mother, wise old woman gaining power, that is, queenliness. The great goddess was simultaneously the mistress of the underworld (virgin), the earth (mother), and the heavens (queen). The three dimensions reflect the phases of the moon: new, waxing, and dying in preparation for renewal. We begin to see the cosmic implications of the goddess energy, the divine feminine. For instance, in some traditions, the earth was considered to *be* the Great Mother. Mary, on the archetypal/metaphorical level, can be seen as a container of the ancient threefold energy that characterized the great goddess.

The excesses of devotion over the past two millennia regarding Mary become more understandable once we see them in the light of the perennially venerated threefold goddess rather than to the Mary of the Gospels. What may seem like idolatry when applied to the woman from Nazareth is, however, quite understandable when applied to her spiritual *meaning* in spiritual consciousness. In fact, no one has yet praised her enough. There can be no excesses for the Source of and the guide to the mystery of the divine life in us and in all the cosmos. Mystically, Mary is the "yes" by which the timeless divine life entered into time. In the following three sections, we will examine each of the three qualities of the divine feminine—virgin, mother, queen—both in ancient pagan times and in the Litany of Loreto.

> *Inciting love in every heart, you bring forth genera-tion after generation.*
> —Lucretius (d. 55 BC), Prayer to
> Venus as Mother of Rome

VIRGIN

O Mary! Allah has chosen thee, and purified thee and chosen thee above the women of all nations.
—Qur'an, Surah 3:42

Beliefs in virgin births were common in ancient times. Many heroes in the Greek world and even Buddha were believed to have been born in a virginal way. Only St. Luke tells of the annunciation. Only he and St. Matthew mention the virgin conception of Jesus. Being a native of the Hellenistic city of Antioch, St. Luke was probably conscious of the power of this archetype in god and hero stories. He often contrasts the kingdom of God to that of the emperor, Augustus. Jesus offers a new society based on love, nonviolence, and liberty unlike that of Rome. St. Luke may have been attempting to show the early Christians that Jesus is a new spiritual Augustus. In the Roman Empire, people commonly believed that Augustus was born of a virgin. His mother was thought to have been impregnated by Apollo in the form of a snake while she slept in the god's temple praying for a son. Augustus was therefore believed to be and was referred to as "the Son of God." St. Luke says, in effect, here is the real God, born virginally as Augustus was, but greater and more reliable than he because he is the ruler of hearts, forming an empire of justice, peace, and love rather than injustice, aggression, and division.

In primitive pagan religion, the goddess was a virgin-mother because the feminine was sufficient in the origin of life, its destruction, and its regeneration. Only in the later patriarchal religions was she the wife/daughter of a god or the earth mother who required a sky father to be a source of fertility.

In the body-negating perspective that so many of us inherited, sex was often considered spiritually dangerous. Mary was above ordinary women because she never engaged in sex, implying that the choice to be sexual was somehow wrong or weak. The virginity of Mary is actually about a much more positive and universal theme in the Savior story: his mother is a virgin, that is, he transcends opposites and overturns nature's laws.

Virginity, in archetypal spiritual parlance, does not refer to a physical condition. Such literalism trivializes the mystery. Mary is not a vestal archetype. She indeed represents the virgin archetype, but she is also the mother archetype and the powerful queen archetype. Virginity in the realm of the spiritual psyche refers to the strength and clarity of purpose that opens one to the Spirit/Self so that a new consciousness can be born. Purity in its loftiest significance does not refer to chastity or celibacy. To say Mary is pure means that she is complete. The archetypal Mary is pure and virginal, that is, she is in no need of ego intervention to contact or usher in the Source. Virginity symbolizes independence from the need for mortal intervention, not inhibition of natural drives.

In our Catholic childhood of the 1950s, the almost fanatical emphasis on Mary's purity created a distance between her and us. Once the historical Mary is more human, she becomes the archetypal mirror of our own ever-complete souls. *Virginal* in archetypal terms means "hidden, not yet revealed," like our souls, which remain virginal, intact, all our lives no matter how our bodies change. Full of grace is full of gifts, one of which is purity from ego illusions or fears. At the annunciation, Mary grants a body to the Divine through the gift of her body. Virginity, in this sense, is not antiphysical but expresses a spiritual reality.

Mary's humility at the annunciation is a way of saying that the soul of the virgin archetype is tenanted by God alone not by ego. Only in that way could Mary say yes to something that she does not understand. "How can this be?" becomes "Let it happen." *Mary is full of grace because she is full of yes.* This "yes" was considered passively subservient in our childhood vision of Mary. She was a model of submission in the patriarchal version of her that we inherited. It is time to relinquish that model and see Mary as an active participant in salvation history.

Surrender means resonance with the tune that spiritual wholeness seems to be playing in our lives. The conditions of our existence are the notes of that tune, also called *the will of God*. When control disappears, God appears. Spiritual surrender does not mean giving in. It is not passive or weak.

It takes tremendous power and determination to say yes to what is. It is a gift of grace, but then it is up to us to put it into practice. On the throne of the Chinese emperors were inscribed the words *Wu Wei,* meaning "Do not interfere with what wants to happen."

Our willingness to respond with an unconditional yes to the will of God, to what is, to that which is beyond our control is the essence of sanctity. The archetypal woman we call Mary is the mystery of that willingness and that is why the word *virgin* fits perfectly.

In Islam, only a virgin can open the gates of enlightenment and guide the soul's mystical passage to a higher life. The virgin-mother symbolism in that tradition fits for the Mary we know too. Mary is an honored figure in the Muslim tradition. She is mentioned in the Qur'an more often than in the Bible, and her birth is presented as miraculous.

The Litany of Loreto addresses the Virgin in a variety of ways. We now explore the titles in the Litany regarding Mary as virgin.

The Advent liturgy says, "O wisdom who came out of the mouth of the Most High, reaching from end to end and ordering all things mightily and sweetly, come and teach us the way of prudence." Mary is called a prudent virgin from the Latin word *providential,* which means "to see ahead."

Mary is called *Virgin Most Venerable* and *Virgin Most Renowned* from the Latin word *praedicanda,* "to be preached." It is up to us to spread the word about her wonderful power and energy. In this second millennium, we are ready to restore the place of the feminine divine in religion and human consciousness in general. Mary is here to assist us.

Mary is thus called *Virgin Most Powerful* because of the power of the feminine in nature and in grace. Our ego belief is that the only means for change is effort. To say the virgin is powerful is to say that human effort is no longer all we have going for us. A strong feminine resource of grace, full of grace, is in us and wanting to overflow, to give birth to a consciousness that is loving, wise, and healing.

Mary is rightly called *Virgin Most Merciful* and *Mother of Mercy*. In Hebrew, the word *mercy* in the singular means "womb." In the story of the two prostitutes who found the wisdom of Solomon, we read that the rightful mother pleaded with the kings "because compassion for her son burned within her" (1 Kgs 3:26). The imperative to be merciful as God is merciful is the equivalent of contacting our inner feminine powers. Mother love is unconditional. That is the unique and enduring characteristic of the divine feminine. We are called to be merciful in that same unconditional way. Mary is the model of this and the assisting force in our finding it in ourselves. Prayer to her and the sense of her energy in us works to foster our limitless compassion.

We understand now that all archetypes have a darker side. Dark does not refer to complexion but to what remains unconscious and thereby can become harmful or dangerous. The dark side of the virgin archetype is in the tendency toward scorn for the material world and bodiliness. A commitment to virginity as a consecration to the spiritual life may lead to a despising of nature, the world, and the body. Many saints were caught in a one-sided and body-abnegating lifestyle. This is hiding in a dualism in order to avoid full contact with incarnate reality. Virginity is not an ideal unless it is a choice that makes a person more available to the world as a prayerful and compassionate presence. It is not a refuge from the world because that would be a denial of the incarnation.

Finally, the dark side of the virgin motif may come through as a fear of connection—especially with the unwashed masses. Since St. Thomas describes spirituality as "a connectedness with all things," this is a great peril to our spiritual progress. Virginity is holy—as anything is—when it means not distance, division, or disdain, but all-inclusive caring and closeness. We are here to imitate that connectedness.

Nothing about Mary is meant to be a distant ideal and thereby make her impossible to emulate. As long as she is on a pedestal, some of our own most precious potential and power are lost to us. In full spiritual consciousness, her virginity is the intactness of our own souls. St. Ambrose, commenting on the Magnificat, states, "In the heart of each one may Mary praise the Lord, in each may the spirit of Mary rejoice in the Lord."[3] Thus, Mary sings her Magnificat in us; this is what is meant by the virginity of Mary alive within us. Ever-virgin is the name of our souls.

> *When God decided to realize His Incarnation before our eyes, He had first of all to raise up in the world a virtue capable of drawing Him as far as ourselves. He needed a mother who would engender Him in the human sphere. What did he do? He created the Virgin Mary, that is to say He called forth on earth a purity so great that, within this transparency, He would concentrate Himself to the point of becoming a little child. There, expressed in its strength and reality, is the power of purity to bring the divine to birth among us.*
> —Pierre Teilhard de Chardin, *The Divine Milieu*

Prayer

Virgin Mary, tug at my soul and bring me to you.
Open my heart to surrender to the givens of my life
no matter how difficult.
I am thankful that everything that happens to me is
leading me to a new birth of love in my heart,
wisdom in my choices, and healing in my life.
Mary let me be, like you, a channel and a resource of
this love, wisdom, and healing.
Be with me as I give to everyone without exception
the gifts that you give me.
May the openness you call forth in me become my
openness to others, not only near and dear but far
and wide.
May the surrender you teach me become my
dedication to God, visible to me in the needs of
the world.
May my choices be pure and universe-directed.
Let me consent to the compassion and communion
you ask of me.
Never let me miss an opportunity to respond to the
callings of the Holy Spirit.
May I always let you bring me, and all of us, to your
single-hearted annunciation love.

MOTHER

*The Mother of Songs, the mother of our whole seed,
bore us in the beginning. She is the mother of all
races and the mother of all tribes. She is the mother*

*of the thunder, the mother of the rivers, the mother
of the trees, and of all things. She is the mother of
songs and dances. She is the mother of the older
brother stones. She is the mother of the grain and the
mother of all things. She is the mother of the ani-
mals…and the mother of the Milky Way. It was the
mother herself who began to baptize….And the
mother has left a memory in all the temples. With her
sons, the saviors, she left songs and dances as a
reminder….*
—Song of the Kagaba Indians, Columbia, Canada

In ancient Greece, childbirth and preparation of the
dead for burial were in the hands of women. Our life story
thus mythically begins and ends with feminine caretaking.
Indeed, all spiritual and physical growth requires a relationship to a mother. That relationship contains all the phases of
human life from that of a physical mother to a growing
appreciation and kinship with Mother Nature and then to
our spiritual mother at rebirth. We are here on earth not
only because we were born but in order to be born. We
invoke Mary as a mother because we know at some deep level
that she can help us be born spiritually. Like our death, our
birth has not happened fully yet. We invoke her also at the
hour of our death for a rebirth. Such a prayer is not new to
human consciousness. The ancient Greek Orphic Death-
Resurrection Ritual says, "I have entered the bosom of
Persephone, Queen of the Underworld."[4] This is a way of
acknowledging the necessity of a return to the Divine
Mother for rebirth, as we also return to our Earth Mother at
death in preparation for resurrection.

In *The Flowing Light of the Godhead,* the mystic St.
Mechtild of Magdeburg hears Mary dub herself that spiri-

tual mother of all humankind: "I suckled the prophets and sages before God was born." Juliana of Norwich, in *Revelations of Divine Love*, proclaimed the motherhood of God and also said, "Our Lady is our mother in whom we are all enclosed...and our savior is our mother in whom we are endlessly born....To motherhood belong nature, love, wisdom, and knowledge, and this is God." She summarized the entire mystic teaching. Mystics and visionaries spoke in just such archetypal language. More women than men were mystics. In practical terms, they had more time because they were not allowed to have clerical duties. They were thought to be eccentric but that was because they were such a minority. Mystics were suspect in the medieval Church also because authorities suspected that mystical contemplation was a cover for rejection of the need for the Church and its rituals. In a way, this was a legitimate fear from their point of view since, in contemplation, God is indeed discovered to be present in and as our own interior life!

We cherish the Great Mother of whom Mary is our familiar and traditional personification. Yet describing God as father or mother is functional, not ontological. The words do not define but present metaphors for the creative and sustaining dimensions of the divine life—the same as the deepest reality of our humanity and that of nature.

All we have are metaphors for the mystery of that unity. Even the word *God* is a personification since, as we have heard, God is more unlike anything than like anything. We were brought up with a belief in God as the Trinity. Father and Son refer to relationships not persons. The Holy Spirit, as feminine, expresses mother energy. We notice that both Mary and the Holy Spirit appear at the annunciation. Both are needed to combine the spiritual and the human so the human-divine incarnation can happen. They are both necessary for the epiphany of the full mother archetype.

As we have noted, the dark side of the divine mother is not harmful but it is painful. She challenges us by tipping us out of the nest of comfort into the free-fall world with all its demands. She insists that we grow up. At the same time, she is present in every phase of our spiritual development but never as a crutch, only as a resource.

A dark side of a biological mother comes to the fore when she suffocates us in her embrace, thereby preventing us from launching and developing, making filiation a debt that engenders guilt, and violating our boundaries under the pretext of watching over us. These qualities of some mothers are present in the archetypal mother when we concentrate too much on exalting her and having recourse to her without also finding her strength in ourselves. That is the balance that helps us face the shadow of any archetype.

Finally, we notice and appreciate the caring help that has always been included in the mother archetype personified by Mary. Here are verses from a Gaelic hymn of the thirteenth century:

> There is no hound in fleetness or in chase,
> Nor wind nor rapid river,
> As quick as the mother of Christ to the bed of the
>   dying....

My son Josh, at age twenty-one, traveled to Venice and saw there the radiant picture *Assumption of the Virgin* by Tiziano. He showed me a postcard of the painting. I remember him saying as we were both looking at it, "Look how it shows Mary rising up *quickly* into heaven." I thought then, she wanted to start helping us as soon as she possibly could.

The traffic between heaven and earth from the incarnation to the assumption is about this loving zeal of the divine for our humanity. That is the zeal to which we are also called.

Rapidity of succor is associated with the divine mother in many cultures. For instance, in tantric Buddhism, Tara is the mother of the Buddhas. As a female bodhisattva—the enlightened one who is committed to helping others find enlightenment—she moves rapidly, like a woman immediately responsive to her child's cries. Tara symbolizes the light that makes all beings Buddhas. She has a dark side also. It is Maya, the one who created samsāra, the cycle of fear and grasping. Thus she represents a combination of light and shadow. In her red, yellow, and blue raiment, she is the goddess in her threatening aspect; in her green and white garb, she is the gentle and nurturing mother. Her name means "leads across"—from samsāra to nirvana. She redeems and connects the two planes, mortal and immortal.

Tara is also described as moved with compassion for the souls in hell, and she releases them in an instant. She thus terminates all separations, another power of the divine feminine. The name *Tara* means "she who hears—or *is*—the cries of those who are suffering in hell and comes to them quickly." She is a personification of the feminine energy in the higher Self that hears the cries of the ego beset by fear and clinging. Thus the power of enlightened compassion for suffering is within us as is the dark hell realm of suffering itself. We see this combination in many traditions: "I am the queen of all divine powers and of hell and heaven," Isis says in *The Golden Ass* by Apuleius. Heaven and hell in the archetypal world are interior domains of the psyche.

These descriptions of the divine feminine help remind us of Our Lady of Mount Carmel pictured as releasing souls from purgatory. The pious belief that she would release a devotee from purgatory by the Saturday after his or her death is another way of commenting on the swiftness of the divine mother to be our helper. These promises and mythologems are not meant to be taken literally lest they become superstitions. They are acknowledgments of the quality of speed and compassion in the feminine archetype, common in all religious traditions. Thus we notice how, at Cana, Mary accelerated the entry of Jesus into his public life. There is even a title of Mary as *Our Lady of Prompt Succor*, the patroness of New Orleans and Louisiana.

Here is an equivalent in a twelfth-century poem to Mary:

> Thou hast helpen me in many ways
> And brought me out of Hell to Paradise.
> I thank for it, beloved Ladye,
> And I will thank thee for it while I live.

I end this section sharing an experience I had while looking at a picture of the Madonna in a church in Rome. Mary was shown smiling at the infant Jesus and holding him in a joyous cuddling embrace. I felt her warmth in that moment and was so touched that I spontaneously prayed to Mary, "Hold me that way." I think it was the best prayer I ever said to her.

The Madonna and Child are God's supreme truth.
—Michelangelo

Prayer

Mother of beginnings and endings, be with me today and every day of my life.

Mother of endless grace, form me and reform me so
I can be born and reborn.

Launch me into the way of Christ. Bring Christ to
birth and resurrection in me.

I trust that you are here with me and nurture me in
ways I cannot fully comprehend or imagine.

You love me and show me how to live with trust in
this changing world. You are the changes. You are
the constancy.

May all that I do and feel today be useful to you in
your cosmic-wide work for the spiritual evolution
of all creation.

May all that I pray for and all my spiritual practice
become useful to my brothers and sisters who long
to be born and reborn but may not have found the
light of your gentle path.

May I be motherly in my love and cherish the
motherly love of nature and of you.

I commend to your maternal instincts all those I love
and all beings far and wide.

Come quickly when I find myself in a hell of fears.

Let me rise with you into the heaven of freedom
from fear and freedom for love.

QUEEN

*The crown and halo are symbols of the Self, of whole-
ness….The ego is doing on earth what Christ is doing
in heaven…crowning the Virgin Mary. The principle
of materiality and egohood is being glorified: an ego
that is consciously living out the process of continu-
ing incarnation.*

—Edward Edinger, *The Christian Archetype*

We now explore the titles in the Litany regarding Mary as queen, that is, as one having power to help us evolve spiritually in the kingdom of Christ.

An ancient title of the pagan mother goddess was *Queen of Heaven*. Mary holds and preserves this title. As mother of all the living, she is the archetype of the power of the spiritual as it orders and guides the universe. This is an evolutionary and cosmic power that acknowledges the role of the feminine in the ongoing work of creation. Evolution in its feminine dimension is open-ended and ever-newly self-organizing rather than having a goal already planned out. It is an imaginative process, not a fixed schema. It is open, not closed; unfolding, not folded up.

Such openness will be threatening to a strictly patriarchal society. A culture dominated by males will fear the divine feminine as a competitor to the one God. A partnership society, on the other hand, will see the Divine in male and female forms and in all of nature as well. Jeremiah fulminated against the women of Israel who said, "We will do everything that we have vowed, make offerings to the queen of heaven and pour out libations to her, just as we and our ancestors, our kings and our officials, used to do in the towns of Judah and in the streets of Jerusalem" (Jer 44:17).

In Catholic Tradition, the Litany of Loreto honors the specific domains of Mary's queenship. She is queen of the patriarchs Abraham, Isaac, and Jacob. This title shows the time-transcending nature of the higher Self and how it establishes and survives as a continuity throughout the generations. The patriarchs lived in the distant past, and yet their covenants still abide. They continue to guide us. They are our spiritual ancestors, and Mary is the queen of all of us—the new Eve who rules the world of spiritual promise.

She provides and protects our inheritance of evolutionary wisdom.

As queen of prophets, Mary enters the present and the future. The prophetic spirit was strongly at work at the annunciation and nativity. Zachary, Elizabeth, John in her womb, the shepherds, the Magi, the priest Simeon, all acted as prophets foretelling the glory of Christ. Mary is a prophetess in her Magnificat. She is first poet of the new order and she is herself foretold by the prophets. Mary is the feminine word that makes human flesh the covenant of the ages.

The Hebrew name of the mother of Jesus is Miriam, the daughter of Anne and Joachim. Her name recalls an ancient tradition. In the Hebrew Bible, Miriam is the older sister of Moses. She is a significant figure in the movement to feminize Judaism today. In the Genesis story, Miriam placed Moses in a basket and sailed him down the Nile for his own safety. In Talmudic tradition, she convinced her father to continue building a family when he was frightened by the Egyptian law ordering the death of newborn male Israelites. Miriam is looked upon as a prophetess since she foretold Moses as the savior of Israel. It was Miriam who sang a song of victory with the Israelite women after the crossing of the Red Sea (see Exod 15:20). She is a prototype of Mary who also sang prophetically in her Magnificat.

As queen of confessors—or witnesses—Mary protects and encourages the word that can be spoken by all of us. She was always regarded as the first witness by reason of the traditional belief that she related the story of Jesus' infancy to St. Luke. Mary is present at the beginning of our salvation story—the incarnation. She is present at the beginning of the Church—Pentecost. She is present in us at the beginning, middle, and end of our spiritual journey as our mother, support, and companion.

Mary is queen of martyrs. St. Therese of Lisieux wrote in *The Story of a Soul*, "If one is completely dedicated to loving, one must expect to be sacrificed unreservedly." Mary oversees the sacrifice of the limited ego to the higher purposes of the Self. The ego does not have to die, only be deconstructed and reanimated in a renewed, reborn condition. This is the painful process of *kenosis*, Jesus' self-emptying at the incarnation. We are reminded of the necessity of ego-emptying for spiritual realization. This was the purpose of asceticism by the saints, although they often took it too literally and harmed their bodies in the process.

Second Isaiah (chapters 40—55) showed the Israelites the deeper meaning of being the chosen people. It is not about being above others but about a calling to serve humanity through their own suffering. Isaiah sees suffering as redemptive. Thus, he says of the servant-messiah, "Surely he has borne our infirmities and carried our diseases; yet we accounted him stricken, struck down by God, and afflicted" (Isa 53:4). This is a powerful statement of the condition of existence that suffering has the power to bring about growth and renewal. When we join our own suffering to Christ's redemptive purpose, we find the grace of irrepressible courage. We can offer our suffering and courage for the good of all beings. This is how the mystery of the cross becomes part of our life.

As queen of virgins, Mary is the archetypal feminine that contains and is the Source. She offers direct access to the Source by showing us how it is our essential being. When our ego is free of fear and grasping, we are one with her. Then we acknowledge the Source in ourselves and begin sharing its resources of compassion and joy, as the apostles did on Pentecost. They shared themselves as resources once they were purified of fear. Freedom from fear is contact with the Source.

Mary is queen assumed into heaven. To say she was assumed body and soul, from the Jungian/archetypal point of view, is to say that wholeness is indestructible, exempt from the limitations imposed by time or age. Mary's assumption is a prototype of our destiny as humans to combine grace and bodiliness.

Perhaps we have not yet personally believed in the full implications of the incarnation since we have limited it to Christ as an individual and not so much to him as the Mystical Body of the universe. Pierre Teilhard de Chardin writes of this in *The Divine Milieu*: "The only subject ultimately capable of mystical transfiguration is the whole of humankind forming a single body and a single soul in love."

All humans were and are transcendent and eternal as well as embodied and temporary. We do not attain immortality, only discover it as a grace. That is a feminine process since it is not based on logic or human effort.

The immaculate conception tells us when Mary became the special candidate of the archetype: from the very beginning she was meant to contain the pure Source without dependency on ego intervention, that is, by the power of grace. In Jungian terms, the immaculate conception is a way of saying that Mary, our heavenly mother, is free of the corruption by the inflated ego symbolized by the choice of Eve, our first earthly mother.

The archetypal Mary reconfigures the conditions of existence that have been thought of in our traditional teaching as the results of "original sin." Yet, with this new perspective, the painful givens of life can be considered not penalties but *difficult blessings* since they are the challenges we face on our heroic journey. Yet we are always assured of graces sufficient for dealing with them. They can be our escorts to knowing our true nature: if our deepest reality is divine, then the conditions of existence are divine graces since they give us depth, which is precisely where we find the divinity in ourselves. The givens of our existence do not close the gates of Eden. They are actually the gate-keepers of spiritual awakening. The givens of human nature hurt us and try us *while* they make us stronger. They are a product of growth and a price of growth. They are not obstacles but footholds on the spiritual ascent. *Since every event in life, without exception, offers us an opportunity for grace, reality itself is holy.*

We find another dimension in the Eden archetype: Riane Eisler points out that in Genesis, "it is not Cain's killing of his own brother Abel that condemns humanity to live forever in sorrow; it is, rather, Eve's unauthorized or independent 'taste' of what is evil or good."[5] Our theological tradition shows its patriarchal bias when it configures the original sin to be a woman's disobedience, based on curios-ity, rather than a man's sin of fratricide, based on hate.

In the archetypal perspective, original sin refers to the innate presence of the shadow, a darkness in us that we inherited and did not cause. It is comprised, mainly, of three self-deceptions: It is an inflated belief in entitlement to an exemption from the conditions of existence. It is an inborn inclination to be driven or stopped by fear or greed. It is a habitual choice to punish and retaliate when we are hurt and to run or betray when we are loved.

Original sin is also a way of referring to the inflated ego that rejects an axis with the spiritual Self. Thus the phrase "conceived without original sin" is yet another indication that the Mary we honor is an archetype, that is, a personification of the Self, free of ego deceptions. Immaculate conception is indeed immunity from deception.

The title *Queen of the Rosary* was added to the Litany of Loreto in 1614 by the Dominican order. It became official under Pope Leo XIII in 1883. The Rosary is not a superstitious ritual. It emanates from an ancient religious consciousness. A rosary is referred to in the *Bhagavad Gita* 7:7, where the string is the Atman or higher Self that holds all things together. The prayer on each bead corresponds to breaths. This Hindu rosary is sacred to Sarasvati, the goddess of language. Hence it has fifty beads for the fifty letters of the Sanskrit alphabet. The goddess hears the words of the prayers and is the Word. The Buddhist rosary has 108 beads. This is twelve times nine, to represent the cycles of the universe. The Muslim rosary has thirty-three beads for the ninety-nine names of God. In all instances, the rosary is a prayer wheel and a living mandala, a symbol of wholeness.

Blessed Alan de la Roche, a Dominican of the fifteenth century, introduced the Rosary to Catholics. In 1479, Pope Sixtus IV commended it as a devotion. It was called *The Psalter of the Poor* because the 150 Hail Marys represented the 150 psalms. In 1557, Pope Pius V, a Dominican, recommended it as the prayer for a Christian victory at Lepanto. The victory was won on October 7, which became the liturgical feast of the Rosary.

Queen of Peace is the title appended by Pope Benedict XV in World War I. "Blessed are the peacemakers" (Matt 5:9) is a reference to the feminine pacific quality of our higher Self, so unlike the bellicose ego that thrives on discord and competition. The style of the feminine is the foundation for peacemaking, a primacy granted to unconditional love, wisdom, and healing power. This is the opposite of military, retaliatory, and warlike styles of behavior.

In Greek mythology, Mars, the god of war, and Venus, the goddess of love, produce a daughter and name her Harmony. Peace is the harmony of masculine and feminine, a warrior spirit for justice and a heroic soul for mercy.

May 31 is the Feast of the Queenship of Mary. Here is a striking passage from the Third Nocturn of Matins of that feast. It was written by St. Bonaventure and affirms some of the themes of this book:

> Mary the Queen outshines all others in glory, as the Prophet clearly shows in the Psalm which particularly concerns Christ and the Virgin Mary. It first says of Christ, "Thy throne, O God, stands forever and ever," and shortly thereafter of the Virgin, "The queen takes her place at Thy right hand," that is, in the position of highest blessedness, *for it refers to the glory of soul.* The Psalm continues, "In garments of gold," by which is meant the clothing of glorious immortality which was proper to the Virgin in her Assumption....She is enthroned next to her Son....The Virgin Mary is a most excellent Queen towards her people: she obtains forgiveness, overcomes strife, distributes grace; and thereby leads them to glory.[6]

As we embrace the archetypal perspective, we see that the dark side of the queen archetype is in her power to show us the path so unerringly that we might not realize we have to seek it for ourselves. When the Church becomes the repository of all truth and theologians are silenced for their eccentric hypotheses, the dialogue-crushing ego of the queen appears. Loyalty to royalty does not mean that we have neither our own intellectual authority nor the right to question or oppose the authority of others. Yet that can happen to us when the archetype of queen is overly emphasized. Then we become pawns of power, not sharers in it. This inequality is toxic to the human spirit, the only spirit that can incarnate the Spirit of God. A hierarchy that rules unilaterally rather than shares power collegially and serves is the shadow of the queen archetype and the shadow of power in all its forms.

The dark side of the queen archetype also appears in the loyalty she may demand of us. We may be so possessed by her sway over us that we believe it necessary to surrender our uniqueness, our exuberance, or our freedom. A spiritually authentic surrender includes choice *and* self-assertion. Once we trust that the divine life is within us, we are no longer self-abasing. We realize then that spiritual progress means self-realization, not blind obedience.

The dark side is not malicious. It appears when it is ignored or projected so we can get back on track. It is a signal that it is time to rebalance when we have become one-sided or are in denial of the potential in any reality—including God—for error or for extremism. It holds creative possibilities and graces when we work with its energy. We recall Isaiah: "I will give you the treasures of darkness and riches hidden in secret places" (45:3). The shadow side of the queen, like all shadow energy, can ultimately help us find our voice and our power as coworkers in the evolution of love, wisdom, and healing in the world.

Prayer

Mary, Queen of Heaven and Earth, I serve you with
all my powers and gifts.

This is why I have them.

I show everyone in my life and in the world around
me your royal road of love.

May your presence in my life help me let go of my
ego with all its arrogance and with all the fear that
drives it.

May I depose that empty power in favor of the real
power in life which is to place my gifts at your
service.

I offer myself as completely as I can in this moment.

I want to be a courier of your gentle and guiding love
in the world.

Rule my mind with wisdom when I am overcome by
confusion.

Let my mind be a conduit of your truth.

Rule my body with clear purpose when I am at the
mercy of untamed impulses.

Let my body be the instrument of your freedom.

Rule my soul with healing when I am depressed and
forlorn.

Let my soul be the channel of your joy.

Rule my heart with love when I am afraid to love
fully.

Be the queen and guide of my life.

Our very body is a Mary with a Jesus inside.

—Rumi

CHAPTER FOUR

The Mystical Titles of Mary and of Our Souls

Our basic core of goodness is our true self....The acceptance of our basic goodness is a quantum leap in our spiritual journey. God and our true self are not separate. Though we are not God, God and our true self are the same thing.

—Thomas Keating, *Open Mind, Open Heart*

In the mystic view, there is one reality. It is identified as human with respect to us, as natural with respect to the world, and as divine when it refers to God. Mythical symbols and images are expressions of this unity. They have remained intact for all time and still contain their original power. Mythic images can serve a transformative function, like the mother archetype itself, by recreating and repairing our fragmented wholeness. We fragment when we lose touch with the far-reaching dimensions of our spiritual identity: human, natural, and divine.

The titles of the Litany of Loreto are spontaneous images arising from the collective soul of religious consciousness. Carl Jung wrote in *Answer to Job*, "The religious need longs for wholeness and therefore lays hold of the images of wholeness offered by the unconscious, which, independently of the conscious mind, rise up from the depths of our psychic nature."[1]

Images—as opposed to logical explanations—are feminine. Perhaps the iconoclastic fever of the eighth and ninth centuries, Protestant iconoclasm in the sixteenth century, and rejection of images in fundamentalist religion today are, at root, forms of antifeminism. The feminine is associated with imagistic impression as the masculine is associated with logical and verbal clarity. If God is strictly a male force, then we humans are not made in the image of wholeness. Theologically, God has no gender. Yet, we easily personify God as male and adore him as such. At the same time, we are quick to make it clear that we do not adore any female personification of God. One wonders how much of that is theological accuracy and how much is based on the antifeminism of patriarchy. In any case, the mystical tradition in religions across cultures restore and honor the feminine divine.

Imagination is an organ of prayer because images may work better than words or thoughts to convey divine/human union. This is expressed by Lucius, the hero of *The Golden Ass* by Apuleius, when he admits his inadequacy in praising the Egyptian mother goddess, Isis, if he uses only his intellect: "Nevertheless, poor as I am, I will do as much as I can in my devotion to you; I will keep your divine countenance always before my eyes and the secret knowledge of your divinity locked in my heart."[2] Notice that the image is in an inner shrine, an interior refuge. Imagination has brought the goddess into—and up from—his psyche in an enduring and nurturant way.

We will now explore fifteen individual images of Mary, the most touching and poetic titles in the Litany of Loreto. They escort us into the realm of the divine feminine. I include insights into the dark side of each title so that we can gain a fuller picture of its meaning. This part of the book is more devotional in character than the previous parts and is more for meditative reading. As before, each is followed by a prayer.

MIRROR OF JUSTICE

The eye by which I see God is the same as the eye by which God sees me. My eye and God's eye are one seeing, one knowing, and one loving.
—Meister Eckhart, Sermon IV

In Jungian psychology, the anima, the soulful feminine archetype, serves as a mirror function in the psyche. In the depths of the psyche is the God archetype and that includes Mary as the feminine mirror image of the male side of God. This is a living metaphor since the Divine is not caught in human dichotomies and actually has no opposing sides, only energies that continually interconnect. The Divine is the life in us that transcends divisions.

At the incarnation, Mary found a Source *within*, that is, she is the mystic who mirrors God—the interior life of herself. When we humans look for God, we discover that our souls are mirrors of divine life. When we seek God, we are finally looking at ourselves.

"Mirror mysticism" was prevalent in the thirteenth century. St. Clare, in her letters to St. Agnes of Prague, wrote of Christ as though he was a "mirror without blemish," and that she study her own face in that mirror in prayer:

> Place your mind before the mirror of eternity!
> Place your soul in the brilliance of glory!
> Place your heart in the figure
> of the divine substance
> and through contemplation
> transform your entire being
> into the image
> of the Godhead Itself.[3]

This mirror metaphor of St. Clare is not new; it is a feature of mature religious consciousness the world over. We find a similar concept in Hinduism on the feast of Vishnu. The ritual for that day recommends to the devotee, "Close your eyes and direct your face to the altar. When you open your eyes, look into the mirror. You will see not yourself but your mother or grandmother who will say: 'Repeat your mantra and when you open your eyes and look into the mirror you shall see God.'" This ritual strongly resembles a dialogue between St. Teresa and the Christ child, in which Jesus says, "Who are you?" "I am Teresa of Jesus," she replies, "and who are you?" He answers, "I am Jesus of Teresa."[4]

Thus prayer, in a mystical perspective, means access to the vast space/inner place, where we contain what we pray to. In the Jungian view, it is looking into a mirror that reflects our essential wholeness without interference by our ego conditioning. We see a similar view about prayer in Buddhism from Chogyam Trungpa in *The Tibetan Book of the*

Dead: "The word…translated as prayer means, literally 'wish-path.' It is not a request to an external deity, but a method of purifying and directing the mind. It acts as inspiration by arousing the mind's inherent desire for good, which attracts the fulfillment of its aim."[5]

The liturgy for the Feast of the Immaculate Heart of Mary states, "For she is a breath of the power of God, / and a pure emanation of the glory of the Almighty; / therefore nothing defiled gains entrance into her. / For she is a reflection of eternal light, / a spotless mirror of the working of God, / and an image of his goodness" (Wis 7:25–26).[6] Thus, Mary is also a mirror reflecting wholeness—sanctity.

The metaphor of a mirror refers to images and imaging. Archetypal images are mirrored to us in litany titles as well as in religious figures, people, events, imagination, art, and intuitions. Dreams mirror to us the features of ourselves that await our attention. Interestingly, in this context, Carl Jung said in his Seminar of 1925, "Dreamwork releases an experience that grips or falls upon us as from above, an experience that has substance and body such as those things which occurred to the ancients. If I were to symbolize it, I would choose the Annunciation."

To let an image speak to us is thus a path to a spiritual vision. This receptive style of imagining does what sacraments and rituals do. It lets us see through the existential literal reality of daily life into an essential wholeness. It is a mystical reality we participate in rather than one we merely observe. In fact, it is precisely through our imagination that we participate in the ongoing creation of the world: "He made them in his own image"—God *imagined* us and our world. We continue that creative process prayerfully when we use our imagination in our practice of meditation on the life of Christ.

The titles in the Litany of Loreto arouse our imagination because they are comprised of images. In this combination, everything in our experience and in our feelings becomes centered—brought into harmony.

To let our imagination be moved by the titles of Mary is a form of prayer to her since the full release of imagination requires a surrender. It is the surrender of ego with all its tried and trusty weaponry, attachment to logical left-brain thinking, and rigid mindsets that configure the world in limited and often fear-based ways. All great changes and advances began in the imagination—as did every title in the Litany of Loreto.

Imagination, a feminine power, is to the soul what thinking is to the brain. Imagination looks into things to find a personal truth since the whole truth reveals itself in the objective and the personal, one mirrored reality. To receive that revelation and to abide in it is what is meant by transformation. Imagination is thus the key to transformation because by it, we evoke into consciousness what was hidden in our unconscious. Indeed, transformation is always waiting for us where apparent opposites show themselves to be related as complementary, that is, as mirror images.

Imagination is the nature and activity of the soul, the point of meeting between the ego and the Self. Novalis uses this mirror analogy in *Fragments*: "The soul is the meeting place of the inner and outer worlds....It is the point at which they overlap." Images are thus the mirroring links between the microcosm of ourselves and the macrocosm of the universe. Images do not conjure up a connection but expose one that has always and already been there, or rather here.

The process of imagination has a spiraling trajectory, from vision to word to deed. We see a better world; we affirm it into being; we act in ways that make it happen. This is how we move from image to action and become a mirror of justice in the world.

The dark side of the mirror analogy is in our tendency to be seduced by images so that we lose our grounding in the present. This seduction can distract us from direct contact with the reality of our own commitment to justice. We can be lost in imagination and not move into action. Our calling is not simply to know of our unity with the Divine. Mystics who found that out automatically became more socially conscious, more committed to engaged forms of loving to a universal extent.

The shadow side of this title is in its potential for too much emphasis on reflection. It becomes integrated when it leads to a plan of action for the evolution of the world. Then reflection on images becomes reconstruction of the world in the image of justice, peace, and love. That is how the mystical mirror becomes a mirror of justice. In fact, St. Teresa called her great mystical rapture a joke on her unless it was followed up by "a life of love lived now."

God said, "Let us make humankind in our image, according to our likeness."
—Genesis 1:26

Prayer

Mary, let me reflect your love into the world.
May I care about justice so that I act honestly.
May I mirror justice everywhere by standing up for
    truth as God gives me the light to see it.
May I speak truth to power and not be afraid to take
    a stand for fairness.

May I take the part of those who are too weak to defend themselves.

May all that I do, say, and feel reflect your light into any dark time, your concern into any self-centered time, your love into any scary time.

I am thankful that I am reflecting your presence and your caring.

I want to be the mirror of your limitless caring for the cosmos, Mary.

May I restore the world to wholeness by my commitment to justice, peace, and love, here, now, and everywhere.

May I become you in the world.

SEAT OF WISDOM

Sophia is the mercy of God in us. She is the tenderness with which the infinitely mysterious power of pardon turns the darkness of our sins into the light of grace. She is the inexhaustible fountain of kindness, and would almost seem to be, in herself, all mercy. So she does in us a greater work than that of Creation: the work of new being in grace, the work of pardon, the work of transformation from brightness to brightness....The Blessed Virgin Mary is the one created being who enacts and shows forth in her life all that is hidden in Sophia.

—Thomas Merton, *Hagia Sophia*

The word *wisdom* in Hebrew is *hokmah*. *Wisdom* in Greek is *Sophia*. Both these nouns are feminine. *Logos*, the Divine Word incarnate in Christ, is a masculine noun. Logos and Sophia are complementary. Jesus is the Word as well as the Wisdom of God who "became flesh and dwelt among us." Jesus is a personification of the Divine in all of us. Sophia is an ancient symbol of light and a traditional reference to Mary too.

In a letter to Freud in 1912, Jung writes that Sophia is the same ancient wisdom that is found in depth psychology. This restates the central thesis of this book that the divine life, personified by Jesus and Mary, and the depths of our psyche are one and the same life—and what animates nature too.

Sri Aurobindo taught that the Absolute Being has three dimensions: transcendent, cosmic, and individual, and that humans contain the same three elements, a trinity within. The equation is human is to divine as divine is to nature. These are not static energies but dynamic ones. Hence, we can have a developmental psychology, a process theology, and an evolutionary nature. In the Jungian view, Mary is a personification of the feminine in all three of these as Jesus is of the masculine.

The anima is the soul energy that, in its positive aspect, is Sophia and, in its negative aspect, is the destroyer personified in ancient times as Lilith in Judaism, Kali in Hinduism, Mara in Buddhism. The destructive feminine is personified in Greek myth by the witch Medusa who turns hubris-driven men to stone. She halts and disempowers the male ego—as Judith does to Holofernes in the Hebrew tradition.

The positive movement to immortality, on the other hand, is personified by Sophia, who raises consciousness and widens human life. Wisdom is thus a mediating power that grants access to the Divine. The shadow, the Judith energy, is also ultimately an assisting force since it frees ego of its headstrong traits and finds a way to make it useful to the community.

Mary holding Christ in her arms at Bethlehem is the kindly mother. Mary holding the body of Christ at the foot of the cross presides over the painful dissolution of his mortal life. We might say that she midwifes him to new life in both poses. She holds all of us in both those ways from birth to death and all our lives. Thus she presides over the light and the dark of life. In both instances, she holds Jesus and us in the symbol of a throne, the Seat of Wisdom. The wisdom is the realization that our destiny is both to be comforted and to be crucified. Wisdom is likewise the Holy Spirit that restores us to life. Once Christ is our elder brother and Mary is our mother, their destiny is ours.

A central illusion in us is that there is a way to remain separated from our Source. Spiritual awakening is realizing that "I am not far from God; the Beloved is within." This is the ego awakening to itself as non-dual, the Divine as the deepest reality of the human, God as intrapsychic, within us, ever-evolving with us. A dedication to nondualism is having the heart and mind of Christ, another way of saying there is no separation. The source of our fear is the separation we imagine between ourselves and God. Freedom from fear is recollection of and reliance on our unbreakable bond with all that is. The thirteenth-century mystic, St. Mechtild of Magdeburg, wrote that "the rippling tide of love flows secretly out from God into the soul and draws it mightily back to its Source."[7] This return of the ego to its Source is what is meant by finding our true identity in God, both as individuals and as members of the human family. It is thus liberation from the illusion of separation.

In the *Divine Comedy*, Dante can only enter heaven by having Beatrice as an escort, not Virgil. The masculine takes him as far as heaven, but the feminine is needed for full entry into and rebirth in the transpersonal world. The feminine is required for the completion of our divine destiny.

Sophia is equated with the *Shekinah* in the Kabbalah. The Shekinah is God present among us, canceling distance. In *Jung on Christianity,* we read, "When John [in the Apocalypse] pictures Jerusalem as the bride, he is probably following Ecclesiasticus. The city is Sophia, who was with God before time began, and at the end of time will be reunited with God through the sacred marriage....The sacred marriage, the marriage of the Lamb with his Bride, which had been announced earlier, can now take place. The bride is the new Jerusalem coming down from heaven."[8]

There is a continuity in ancient tradition that females were the mediators of archetypal wisdom. We see this personified in the priestess at Delphi in Greece or in the Sibyl in Rome. Both had associations with serpents, symbols of resurrection, a creature that became equated with the demonic in patriarchal teachings. We notice a vivid example of this in the story of Adam and Eve in the Garden of Eden.

The emphasis on one God in the Judaic tradition is not only a way of preserving monotheism, it is just as much an exclusion of the feminine principle in divinity. A reading of chapter 44 of Jeremiah, for instance, shows the ferocity of the priestly caste against the mother goddess as Queen of Heaven. The priests could not accommodate the feminine in the Divine.

The goddess in ancient times was sometimes joined in sacred marriage to a bull, a symbol of male power. In medieval times, the bull became the horned devil and witches were thought to be his consorts. Healthy instances of this alternative ancient sacred marriage image/ritual of the goddess and the king can be found in the sacred marriage of Yahweh and Sophia or of Christ and the Church in mature Judeo-Christian traditions. The sacred marriage is a metaphor for the ego/Self axis, Jung's description of our individuation, an integration of the psychological and spiritual.

In addition, Jung offered this depth psychology comment on the occasion of the definition of the assumption in 1950: "One could have known for a long time that there was a deep longing in the masses for an intercessor and mediatrix who would at last take her place alongside the Holy Trinity and be received as the 'Queen of Heaven and Bride of the heavenly court...'.It was recognized even in prehistoric times that the primordial divine being is both male and female. But such a truth eventuates in time only when it is solemnly proclaimed or rediscovered."[9]

Finally, Mary can certainly be imaged as the personification of the wisdom in every human soul. We see an example of how this refers to God and nature too in Proverbs:

The LORD created me at the beginning of his work,
    the first of his acts of long ago.
Ages ago I was set up,
    at the first, before the beginning of the earth.
When there were no depths I was brought forth,
    when there were no springs abounding with water.
Before the mountains had been shaped,
    before the hills, I was brought forth—
when he had not yet made earth and fields,
    or the world's first bits of soil.
When he established the heavens, I was there,
    when he drew a circle on the face of the deep,
when he made firm the skies above,
    when he established the fountains of the deep,

when he assigned to the sea its limit,
    so that the waters might not transgress his
      command,
when he marked out the foundations of the earth,
    then I was beside him, like a master worker;
and I was daily his delight,
    rejoicing before him always,
rejoicing in his inhabited world
    and delighting in the human race.

                                        (8:22–31)

Prayer

Mary, lamp of wisdom, enlighten my path.
May I find the wisdom that is in the heart of God,
    in nature, in Scriptures, in my soul, all one truth.
May I share wisdom generously.
May I greet the dawn of wisdom wherever I go
    and not become lost in the sunset of ignorance.
Free me from prejudice and limitation in my views.
Make me open to all possibilities.
May I find your wisdom everywhere.
You occupy the throne in my inner kingdom
and I am always listening to your wisdom
    in words, in others, in nature, in my soul, and in
    everything.
Speak your wisdom in ways I can best hear.
Free me from deafness to the many voices of wisdom
    that surround me so beneficently.
Let my intuitions be messages from you.
Give me the gift of caring deeply that everyone find
    your wisdom.
Give me the gift of sharing the good news in all I am
    and do.

CAUSE OF OUR JOY

The angel said to them, "Do not be afraid; for see—
I am bringing you good news of great joy for all the
people."

—Luke 2:10

The Irish have a devotion, ascribed to St. Thomas of Canterbury, called the seven comforts of Mary. The devotion consists of seven Hail Marys to share in her joys on earth: the annunciation, the visitation, the nativity, the epiphany, finding Jesus in the temple, the resurrection, and the ascension. According to pious tradition, Mary asked St. Thomas to add seven Hail Marys for her joys in heaven: she is honored above all others; she has purity above the angels; her light illumines heaven; earthlings honor her as the Mother of God; her Son grants what she asks; she can and does give grace; and her glory increases till the end of time. All these joys reflect the themes that have characterized devotion to the Great Mother (Cybele, Gaia, Rhea) throughout recorded history.

Mary is the cause of our joy by her participation in the history of our salvation, prefigured in the Gospel and occurring in real time now when we are saved from bondage to the limitations of ego. The themes of bondage in Egypt and of exile in Babylon are two central motifs in the Hebrew Bible. Bondage is followed by the grace of liberation. Exile ends in homecoming. Both these results are occasions of joy. The idea of a spiritual journey is the background of both themes.

Exile is the metaphor for the alienation that happens when we become stuck in our own needs and desires, separate ourselves from others, and imagine God to be far and away from us. Bondage is the metaphor of being caught in ego fears and cravings for the distant goods we think we require. Joy results from freedom and homecoming. Mary is a guide to these possibilities since all her joys flow from her combining a choice for freedom and surrender of ego.

Mary is likewise the cause of our joy because she brings Jesus, our joy, into the world for us. As theologian, Edward Schillebeeckx, wrote, "Being sad in Jesus' presence is an existential impossibility."[10] (We are in that presence now, right here inside us.) Jesus is the new Moses who joyously leads us out of our bondage in parochialism into the promised land of vast cosmic consciousness. Mary is the cause of our joy because she accompanies us on that spiritual journey with Jesus.

Mary is also the cause of joy *because* she is full of grace, the free gift of spiritual energy and momentum that complements us and shows us the divine potential in ourselves. The cause of joy is in us since wholeness/sanctity is in us, God within us: "For what is our hope or joy or crown of boasting before our Lord Jesus at his coming? Is it not you?" (1 Thess 2:19).

Ramakrishna, a nineteenth-century Hindu priest of Kali, the dark goddess, was a devotee of the divine mother. We read in *Teachings of Sri Ramakrishna*, "The Mother does not love those who just float out into the transcendent. The Mother really loves those who play the game wildly, who go for it." Throughout the centuries, the worship of the divine mother was an uninhibitedly joyous experience. One way this was celebrated throughout Catholic history was by the folk rituals surrounding Mary as the Queen of the May. The singing, the crowning of her image, the festive atmosphere helped open us emotionally, another passageway for archetypal energy.

Joy can be a quality of any experience. Speaking metaphorically, we can say that a rose faces autumn with a joy equal to that felt in spring. She knows she will be reborn though not as this same individual rose. Her joy is precisely in the fact that she is not attached to an identity in any limited or literal way. She has let go of attachment to a separate identity in favor of everlasting oneness. Such letting go is the essence of jubilation.

The shadow side of joy is in the opposite of acceptance of change. It is in believing that joy will last forever, a denial of the condition of nature that all is transient. To say yes to the givens of life is devotion to her. That yes helps us since by it, we let go of our ego clinging, the most inveterate obstacle to authentic joy. This is the joy of equanimity in the midst of shifting predicaments and shifting feelings in a shifting world—what is meant by joy in any circumstance. We then not only accept things as they are; we savor them. The shadow proves to be our ally once we befriend it.

Does this mean we are not to have feelings, to weep for losses, to react to the tears in things? There is a story about the Zen master, Shaku Soen. He wept for a man who had died and his tears were ridiculed by a bystander who said, "Are you not supposed to be beyond reaction to the conditions of existence?" Shaku answered, "It is this allowing of grief which puts me beyond it." Feeling is not opposed to the yes or to a "Thy will be done." It is an adornment of it.

We are creating ourselves moment by moment through the dark and light of relationships, events, feelings, images, and all the phantasmagoria of human life— what Dante in *The Divine Comedy* calls "the little threshing floor that makes us all so ferocious." The soul does not care about the price we may have to pay to arrive at spiritual individuation. If it takes dissolution, that is accepted. If it takes a long silence, that is endured. If it is blessed with rapture, that is welcomed. Joy is an ingredient of any day in which wholeness can unfold and that is every day.

Mary is a personification of a sanctity that may happen in us in a variety of ways. Sanctity is in an unencumbered single-heartedness. That is joy. We embody in daily life the abiding powers in the divine Self, love, wisdom, and healing influence—the same qualities we have revered in Christ and the saints. That is joy. It is in receiving with gratitude the graces that make all this possible. That is joy.

Enjoyment can become our motivation in the spiritual life. There is a long-standing connection between reverence and humor. Compare these two quotations from the Hebrew Bible: "Mephibosheth…fell on his face and did obeisance" (2 Sam 9:6). "Abraham fell on his face and laughed" (Gen 17:17). Can we picture Christ or Mary laughing? If we cannot, we have to ask ourselves if our image of them—and of sanctity—is stunted.

Wholeness is another name of God. Since our life purpose is to be holy/whole as God is holy/whole, our destiny is one of joy. Our religious experience in the Church may have been humorless. It is time to restore the joy of the saints, the whole ones, to our spiritual life. Mary's joy today is in the activation of joy in us here and now. This is how we may add one more heavenly joy to the ones she listed for St. Thomas of Canterbury. It is also how we become saints.

The archetype of the divine feminine is eternal. It is the true cause of a human joy that beckons to us from the beginning of time and never ends. That joy is a motivation for virtuous living. In spiritual maturity, we are not good because we are bullied by a fear of punishment; we are good because we are full of delight.

I have loved you with an everlasting love; therefore I have continued my faithfulness to you....Again you shall take your tambourines, and go forth in the dance of the merrymakers.

—Jeremiah 31:3–4

Prayer

Mary, you are the cause of so much joy in my life
    and in the lives of so many.
For this I thank you.
I am grateful for the joy of liberation from ego.
I am grateful for the joy of saying yes to what is.
I am grateful for the joy of my spiritual practice.
You are the Source of joy and the miracle of
    joy-in-pain.
May I find ways to hold those two in my heart as one.
I cherish the memory of your many joys on earth
    and in heaven.
I see them as promises of what my life can be
    for me.
Joy happens when I love with all my might.
Joy happens when I give myself passionately to my
    destiny and forget myself.
Let these joys happen in me.
May I bring joy to the world as you did long ago
    and as you are doing now.
Help me smile much more than ever.

VESSEL OF SPIRIT

I beheld nothing but the divine power in a manner assuredly indescribable, so that through excess of

> *marveling, my soul cried out with a loud voice: "This world is full of God!"*
> —St. Angela de Foligno,
> *Book of Visions and Instructions*

The theme of this title is containment. Mary is the vessel of safekeeping and incubation. She is the baptismal font of new life. She is the Holy Grail that contains Jesus and us. Mary contains divinity like a *pyx*, a word derived from *buxis*, "box," that holds the Body of Christ. She is the tabernacle, what St. Paul called a "vessel of election." In Judaism, the tabernacle is womblike and contains all of God's revelation that is nonetheless continually unfolding. It is not a binder of old canonical texts but a releaser of new and neverending revelations.

The Great Mother was seen as the container of all that is. A dark side of containing is captivity, in which the feminine energy ensnares us and inhibits us. In this aspect, she crushes independence—a feature taken over, like most of the dark side of the feminine, by the patriarchy. However, our independence is often an inflation of ego, hubris, and it is only then that the dark side of the Great Mother arises. The symbol of the dark side of the feminine is the spider, which traps and destroys her prey. We see this same theme in the story of Hansel and Gretel ensnared by the witch mother. (Addiction is an example of a self-chosen visit to the dark vessel of captivity.)

The Egyptian goddess of the sky is Nut. Her image, with embracing arms, was painted in a sarcophagus so she could "hold" the dead body and thereby prepare it for resurrection. The Great Mother was seen in many traditions as holding us in the container of a grave, the incubator of rebirth. We see this in Christian iconography in the *Pietà* in which Mary holds the dead body of Jesus in preparation for Easter. In every image of the ancient Great Mother, we see Mary. In all this, death is a metaphor for the dissolution of ego and the resurrection that follows. In Christian liturgy, the baptismal font serves as a symbol of the vessel in which we enter the water in the womb of the Great Mother to be reborn as children of God.

Mary is called a *Vessel of Spirit*, a *Vessel of Honor*, and the *Singular Vessel of Devotion*. These titles were added to the Litany in medieval times when alchemy was popular. Alchemy was not literally about transforming lead into gold. The vessel in which the leaden ego is transformed into the gold of spiritual wholeness is the spiritual enterprise represented by the science of alchemy. The Litany avers that the alchemical transformation that is our spiritual destiny can happen in the body of the divine feminine, that is, in the cosmos.

In the metaphor of the alchemical vessel, we encounter the two maternal themes of forming and transforming. We see Mary then as the vessel of gestation of Christ and of all of us. She is also the spiritual vessel in which opposites combine. The painful process of letting go of self-centeredness occurs so that the gold of God-centered wholeness can appear.

In Tibetan Buddhism, the peacock is the symbol of the bodhisattva—an enlightened person who chooses to sacrifice himself for others—because it was believed that he ate poisonous plants and transformed them inside himself so that they became his colorful plumage. In medieval times, the peacock was a symbol of resurrection, and its flesh was regarded as an antidote to poison. We likewise, in Hebrews, see a similar reference to Christ "who for a little while was made lower than the angels, now crowned with glory and honor because of the suffering of death, so that by the grace of God he might taste death for everyone" (Heb 2:9).

In Buddhist teaching, Maitreya, the bodhisattva of love, is pictured holding a vessel containing the waters of enlightenment. He waits to sprinkle the world until it is at its worst ebb of delusion and violence. Only then is the world ready for transfiguration. This is another way of seeing how light dances with shadow so that harmony can result.

Vessels contain elixirs and love potions that are also symbols of transformation, often with dark overtones. Yet, the stories of witches and potions were always about a spiritual rebirth, never literal except to those not in the know. A witch is a personification of the negative side of the anima, the female force that dissolves an arrogant ego and transforms us in a painful initiatory way. This is another example of the shadow side of the vessel archetype. To form and contain is a tranquil gift of the good mother. To transform is terrifying because it is challenging, life-changing, and compelling. Mary is not the opposite of the witch but includes her energy. In medieval times when witches were burned and Mary was glorified, Mary was being burned too.

Mary has been honored as the beneficent mother, and witches have been perceived as maleficent women. Now the full archetype can be located in a wider sense of who Mary is. She is too powerful a figure in the imagination of humankind to be cut in half. We can welcome her as the chthonic shadow mother, the feminine transformative power in nature. The two energies of light and dark are in one continuum, and Mary is the archetype that can contain them. This is a recognition of the power of the feminine to embrace the variety of human experience and its destiny of transformation. For example, in ancient Athens, Venus was venerated as the goddess of love; while in Sparta, Venus was the goddess of war. This is not contradictory but an intelligent recognition of the full expanse of an archetype.

A synthesis of dark and light is a requirement in the process of transformation. Thus Mother Nature both feeds us with fruit and poisons us with mushrooms. Waters may drown us or slake our thirst. Earth is our origin and that dust is later what our bodies become. Earth feeds us throughout life, and a hungry earth eats us at death. These are metaphors—like the Litany titles—of a human reality and a divine destiny that thrive in both light and dark.

The Hindu pantheon also reflected unity in diversity. Heinrich Zimmer writes in *Myths and Symbols in Indian Art and Civilization* of the beneficent divine mother *and* of the destructive mother, Kali, as "the dark, all-devouring time, the bone-wreathed Lady of the palace of skulls." This is not meant to be a grim horror but a realistic metaphor of the cost of evolution, the cost of spiritual development, the cost of discipleship. Something feminine abides as an assisting transformative energy in us, always at work. It is the power of grace. Perhaps that is what we have known all our lives as Mary, Mother of Divine Grace.

The divine mother has also been symbolized as shelter in caves, sanctuary in a cathedral, a *temenos*, the sacred space for formation, creation, transformation, ascension—all archetypes of awakening to our spiritual destiny. Mary continually forms and reforms us as we pass through this vale of tears and joy. Seeing her as a vessel is also a way of affirming that we are continually held, that we are not alone or simply out there. We live within, not outside.

A vessel is also *parthenogenic*, a word that refers to virgin birth, since transformation happens within it while it is sealed. This is another pointer to the spiritual meaning of Mary's virginity. The blessing of the baptismal font on Holy

Saturday includes these words: "May a heavenly offspring, conceived in holiness and reborn as a new creation, come forth from the stainless womb of this divine font."[11]

St. Paul reminds us "that each one of you knows how to control your own body [vessel] in holiness and honor" (1 Thess 4:4). How that can happen is summarized in the invocations of the Litany of Loreto and in these meditations on them. A way to fulfill ourselves as unique human beings is by manifesting our talents and finding our bliss. This is how our unique life and gifts become the intact vessel of divine life. We then are hearing our calling to be vessels as Mary was and is. A response to such a call leads to an embodiment of the universal in the unique. Our individuality is an incarnation, that is, an articulation, of Christ in the world.

Finally, we remind ourselves that Mary is called the *Singular Vessel of Devotion.* The word *singular* in Latin is *insigne*—"eminent." Devotion is from the word for *vow.* Our destiny is to be vowed to or consecrated to the twofold graces of Mary: to allow her to form and to transform us in her own way. To be in the vessel of the divine feminine is not to be in control of how it works, but to allow grace to have its way with us no matter which exigencies we may have to deal with as part of the process. We are not only the receivers of graces but the mediators of them to others. This can only happen through humility since "we have this treasure in clay jars [vessels], so that it may be made clear that this extraordinary power belongs to God and does not come from us [ego]" (2 Cor 4:7).

> *Though we are a small vessel, still you have made it full.*
>
> —St. Mechtild of Magdeburg,
> *The Flowing Light of the Godhead*

Prayer

I live my life in the warm vessel of your love, Mary.
You contain me and all my feelings, my thoughts,
  my fears, my hopes, my sufferings, even my
  mistakes.
You are the elixir of change and growth for me.
I say yes to how you transform my leaden ego into
  the gold of loving kindness.
I say yes to how you burn me when necessary and
  then reconstitute me.
I say yes to how you crush me and make me
  "the best wine" for the wedding of all
  humankind.
You are the crucible in which a great change is
  happening in me.
May I remain loyal to this process, however painful it
  may be.
May I emerge from it with an enduring commitment
  to encourage those who are afraid of the fire.
May I remain devoted to you and make my
  contribution to the evolution of the universe
  through all I receive from you.
Devoted Mary, keep pondering me in your heart.

MYSTICAL ROSE

The fairest day that ever yet has shone,
Will be when thou the day within shall see;
The fairest rose that ever yet has blown,
When thou the flower thou lookest on shall be.

—Jones Very, "The Lost"

The alchemical and baptismal theme meets us again in this beautiful invocation. It comes from Sirach 24:18: "I was exalted like the rose of Jericho." That flower is still sold there today. Roses of Jericho are actually dry tumbleweeds that bloom rose-like when placed in water. Thus, they are transformed once they are contained in water, like us at baptism. They thereby summon up the alchemical image of the dark side of the anima: the sirens who dissolve the ego in water so that a spiritual consciousness can emerge. Holy water has this same significance. We sign ourselves with it upon entering a church to transport our head, heart, and shoulders from the ego world to the eternal world.

Goddesses have perennially been associated with flowers. The "rose" in the Hebrew Bible probably refers to a crocus or saffron, hence it is red in the Song of Songs. The blood-red color makes the rose a symbol of resurrection and gives scars and death a mystical significance. This is why roses are placed on graves. Flowers, since they are so short-lived, are intimately connected to the dark side of life—its movement toward death. Flowers, since they thrive in the sun, are intimately connected to the light—the promise of new risen life.

The Mystical Rose can also be a lotus, the symbol of spring, which grew in the Jordan valley in biblical times. Figurines found there show the goddess Astarte holding a lotus. The Buddhist Mother, Tara, holds a lotus stem with three branches in her left hand, representing her three concerns: past, present, and future. Her right hand is open, giving blessings to humanity. Buddha is pictured as the jewel in the lotus, the eastern counterpart of the rose. The lotus rises from the primal muddy waters. This evokes the alchemical theme of perfect beauty from something ugly and unpromising, another symbol of the combination of light and dark in one archetype.

The rose is the mystic center of perfect and unsullied sanctity. The rose is the western symbol of wholeness, and it is also, like the virgin, whole and intact, a flower continuously unfolding. The Cosmic Rose in the Hindu tradition is meant to describe the beauty of the divine mother. The rose window of a cathedral is a mandala of wholeness, a window to another world beyond the ego's narrow and limited vision.

Dante wrote in *The Divine Comedy* of Mary: "Here is the rose in which the word of God was made incarnate." He uses the image of the radiantly blossoming white rose both for Mary and for the beatific vision. This is another reference to Mary as a symbol of the middle world between heaven and earth that simultaneously combines them. *Middle* in this context refers to a linking of the ever-changing and the everlasting. This is the archetypal meaning implied in the term *middle earth.*

Heaven, in the symbolic view, is an image of the Source and destiny of the psyche. It, too, is a rose that combines the feminine light in its blossoms and the feminine dark in its thorns. Where the variations are united, a spiritual direction is being taken. It is a touching synchronous fact that a group of courageously idealistic young people in Nazi Germany formed a resistance movement for which they were all martyred, and it was called "The White Rose."

Angelus Silesius, in the medieval poem "The Romance of the Rose," sees the mystical rose as a symbol of the soul and of Christ's action upon it. The Golden Rose blessed by the pope on the Fourth Sunday of Lent symbolizes his spiritual power. Thus the Mystical Rose shows the spiritual power of the wholeness in which we all participate.

The *Rosalia* was a pagan ritual that took place in May—later to be Mary's month—when roses were offered to the dead. Hecate, the goddess of underworld—the dark side of the anima—was sometimes depicted with a crown of roses. The musical group The Grateful Dead uses this same ancient symbol of roses on the head of a skeleton. In recent times, roses are also a symbol of love with all its thorny vicissitudes, another metaphor for alchemical transformation.

After his vision of Mary at Guadalupe in 1531, Juan Diego was asked by his bishop for a sign. Roses sprung from rocks and he gathered them in his cloak, which also held a picture of the Madonna. Mary was appearing on the spot where formerly there was a shrine to the Aztec goddess, Tonantzin, "our mother," who presided at that very place, even wearing her same colors. This fits with our vision of Mary as one with the Great Mother cherished everywhere and always in the story of humanity.

Apparitions are visions of the spiritual Self granted as cheering graces to the ego along its mortal path. Thus, the vision of the Sacred Heart to St. Margaret Mary displays the unconditional love of God for us. The vision of the Holy Spirit on Pentecost as tongues of fire displays the emboldening wisdom of the Divine that comes to us no matter how much we doubt and fear. The vision of Our Lady of Lourdes displays the healing power of the divine feminine in the midst of nature. It is touching to realize that military personnel and veterans visit the shrine after combat and especially gather there at the annual International Military Pilgrimage—beginning after World War II.

There have been many apparitions of Mary reported since 1900 to people in various religions, including Islam. The Mary who visits the world in apparitions is the archetype of the bodhisattva, the enlightened person who keeps coming back to earth to help others find the light. Unfortunately, the verbal messages of the Madonna in the apparitions reported in the twentieth century have often been fear-based or have fostered superstition. In our new milieu of faith, perhaps messages people hear from Mary will show more openness and zeal for discovery.

The rosary combines three mysterious roses: white, red, and gold. The white rose is joy. The red rose is sorrow. The gold rose is glory. The joyful mysteries of the Rosary are in the leaves of the rose. The sorrowful mysteries are in the thorns. The glorious mysteries are in the petals. They thus each connect with nature.

In addition, the traditional fifteen mysteries concentrate on the bodily experiences of Jesus and Mary. The Rosary is a chain that links the spiritual with the natural and the physical, another reference to the middle world, the domain of the between, always a spiritual realm. Its popularity reflects the wisdom of the psyche: the recognition of how human nature and the divine nature are united. Our Lady of Lourdes, the divine feminine as healer, appeared with a white rose on one foot and a gold rose on the other to show her twin concern with earth and heaven, another joining of the human and the Divine.

Pope St. John Paul II added new mysteries to the Rosary. They are the five mysteries of light: the baptism of Jesus, the wedding at Cana, the public life of Jesus as a teacher and healer, the transfiguration, and the institution of the Eucharist at the Last Supper. These mysteries celebrate the white rose of light that blooms in the life of Christ and are callings to us: we are initiated into the sacramental life, we trust divine power, we hear the Word, we are one with the Christ of glory, we are fed with spiritual food in the sacrament of Christ's body and blood so we can live his risen life in the world. That world is not separate from Eucharist as Pierre Teilhard de Chardin reminds us: "The immense host which is the universe is made flesh."[12]

I was once graced with a visionary dream. I dreamt that a student asked me if the world was getting worse. I said, "No, it is only that its shadow is becoming more richly revealed. It is a mystical rose that is opening, and we are seeing more deeply down into its dark petals."

What God said to the rose, to make its beauty bloom,
He has said to my heart times one hundred.

—Rumi

Prayer

Rose of all my life, I trust you with my past, present, and future.

You are the promise of a renewal of the cosmos that begins today and will cycle throughout all time.

You are the flower of opening and the flower of closing.

You bloom in my heart and I can feel myself expanding.

You bring the thorns that help me become stronger.

You show me how to accept the cycles of change.

May I trust the changes that happen and grow through every one of them.

May I bring the rose of you to everyone I know.

May I find the mystical rose of you in my heart, in nature, and in all my fellow humans.

May I bring the rose of you to all who wander in this garden and may not notice its beautiful blooms.

Be the gardener of what next will bloom for me.

Help me blossom into Christ in the world, Mystical Rose.

TOWER OF DAVID, TOWER OF IVORY

The name of the LORD is a strong tower;
the righteous run into it and are safe.

—Proverbs 18:10

A tower is another example of the "middle world," connecting heaven and earth. The roots of a tower are deep in the earth/nature and thus all three worlds are united: natural, divine, and human.

The tower of Babel was meant to be a ladder to heaven to repair the broken tie between humans and God. The tie is the axis of the human ego and the divine Self that can be restored when people let go of hubris and practice humility. Instead, Babel became a symbol of the inflation of the ego and so led to division and disconnection, what is meant by sin, isolating ourselves from love; all-inclusive caring connection.

Sin is the choice of ego over a life of love, wisdom, and healing. In the perspective of this book, sin is thus an offense against our own true nature. From such ignorance, we obscure the light that is within us. Thus, sin is an obstacle to remove not a stain that shames our soul.

To apply the image of a tower to Mary reflects a long-standing belief in the human psyche that feminine energy has a restorative dimension. It rebuilds the severed unity between us and between us and God. The tie between the human and the Divine cannot be truly broken, since the Divine is the deepest reality of the human psyche. The tie is broken only in the sense that we are no longer conscious of it or committed to acting in accord with it.

Likewise, enlightenment is not something we seek but is already and always in us. We do not become enlightened; we simply notice it at last. Sin is a deliberate obscuration. It takes grace, a feminine archetype, to move us into our full consciousness of the light within us.

Towers were common in the biblical landscape. They were made of brick or stone and were used for refuge from or for defense against armed attack. A large tower was a citadel for the whole village (cf. Judg 9:51; Ps 61:3). Towers sometimes contained wells and were used for the storage of harvests. They were refuges for sheep and workers. Some were military strongholds built into the walls of a city for safety during a siege. This symbology of containment and protection was easily applied to Mary in medieval times. She is not only a tower in the sense of connection between heaven and earth but in the sense of refuge from harm.

In Christian times, the tower was also a symbol of watchfulness and ascent. Towers are observation posts. They take solar energy and distribute it on earth. This is symbolic of a rise in consciousness. Mary is the model of this, since her combination of surrender and choice brought the Divine Word, a higher consciousness, to earth. We are the present-day children of Mary with a messianic purpose, to cocreate a world of justice, peace, and love.

Mary is from the family of David and stands out like a tower since she forecasts the arrival of a messiah. The Litany title *Tower of David* is a reference to an image in the Song of Songs: "Your neck is like the tower of David, / built in courses; / on it hang a thousand bucklers, / all of them shields of warriors" (4:4), and refers to a specific fortress built by David who had recaptured Mount Sion from the

Jebusites and built a tower there. The tower of David was prominently visible to the inhabitants of Jerusalem. From it, warnings could be broadcast if enemies were approaching. By King Herod's time, only the foundation remained, and he built three towers on the site. The strongest of these was called the *tower of David*. It survived the destruction of Jerusalem in AD 70. The tower of David was thus impregnable against the foe, as are we with Mary's help.

The military image of arms and armory fits. Stored in the spiritual tower is the weaponry we need to sanctify ego: virtue and grace. Once we activate goodness—Godness—in ourselves, we find ourselves up against the collective shadow: "For our struggle is not against enemies of blood and flesh, but against the rulers, against the authorities, against the cosmic powers of this present darkness, against the spiritual forces of evil in the heavenly places" (Eph 6:12). It is dangerous to be a saint.

Mary is compared to the tower of David because she is part of a divine defense system in our souls. In her, the kingdom of God—the world of the Self—will stand undefeated, and sin—the choice to succumb to the shadow of ego—will be conquered. Hubris is believing only in the masculine effortful ego and denying its counterpart, the feminine energy of grace. Grace is required in letting go of ego and in moving from arrogance to gratitude.

A tower is a container, the place of formation. This also makes it a fitting symbol of the divine mother. The same archetype appears in the Song of Songs: "I was a wall, / and my breasts were like towers; / then I was in his eyes / as one who brings peace" (8:10).

A soporific contentment can result from containment. That is the dark side of the tower archetype. It can prevent us from finding our journeyer energy, our warrior energy, our courage for direct engagement with life's challenges. When Mary becomes too much of a refuge, we can be lost in an "ivory tower." Our calling is to know when to enter the tower and when to emerge from it.

The Litany image of the Tower of Ivory further shows the feminine side of the archetype. This term is used in the Song of Songs to describe the beauty of the beloved bride: "Your neck is like an ivory tower" (7:4). The psalmist images the bride of the Messiah in an ivory palace filled with music: "From ivory palaces stringed instruments make you glad" (Ps 45:8).

In the Hebrew tradition, the *Zohar*, the book on the Kabbalah, a mystical tradition of Judaism, describes the divine life as having ten spheres, *sephirot*, each with both a masculine and feminine side. Likewise, the Sabbath is referred to as a bride in Judaism. In some rabbinical texts, the creation occurred precisely *for* the Sabbath. It was not God's sabbatical but his purpose. The feminine archetype represents a purpose of humanity and of nature: to stand out like a tower and to be a reliable refuge in a world of illusion and distraction. It is not a sanctuary of stone but of soul. It is not granted to us because of our efforts or merits, but because we are loved by a Love that is unconditional.

> *For not by their own sword did they win the land,*
> *nor did their own arm give them victory;*
> *but your right hand, and your arm,*
> *and the light of your countenance,*
> *for you delighted in them.*
>
> —Psalm 44:3

Prayer

Mary on earth as you are in heaven,
restore the connection between heaven and earth.
Show us heaven on earth as you showed your Son to
    humanity.
Heal the separation that has happened to us:
Let us find divinity in humanity and in nature.
Be our citadel against the powers of evil that rise
    against us sometimes.
May our love transform them and bring out the love
    in them, a love that is real but now hidden
    by fear.
Be our support in times of stress and neediness.
Be our refuge when we are attacked and misunder-
    stood.
Help us stand outside the tower long enough to find
    our strength.
Support us with the strength to face what life brings
    and not to lose heart.
Support us with an armory of love and peace.
May we become your peacemakers.
May we go out into the world and stand out as towers
    for those who need light and safety.

HOUSE OF GOLD

*I remained...in the temple, enjoying the ineffable
pleasure of contemplating the goddess' statue,
because I was bound to her by a debt of gratitude so
large that I could never fully repay her.*

—Apuleius, *The Golden Ass*

Mary is what we are: a temple of the Divine. In this title, we have two symbols, the house as a container and gold as the supreme value in our true nature, our higher Self. The house of gold is that Self. A house grants shelter, and so in this title, we again encounter the conserving and containing aspect of the female archetype. There are always graces to help us integrate those two.

The Loreto shrine, the traditional house of Mary, is like the ark of the covenant, the dwelling of the feminine aspect of God. At sunset, it is bathed in gold, and so it is often referred to as the golden house. It has been visited by pilgrims since medieval times, among them Sts. Ignatius, Francis de Sales, Charles Borromeo, and Alphonse Liquori. Pope St. John XXIII visited it just before convening the Second Vatican Council. John XXIII was the first pope to visit Loreto since the loss of the Papal States in 1870 and ending the idea of the pope as a "prisoner of the Vatican." He came one week before convening the Second Vatican Council and revealed the purpose of his trip: "We have come here to invoke you [Mary] as the first Star of the Council, as the propitious light on our way which winds faithfully towards the great ecumenical assembly of universal expectation." He goes on to summarize the importance of Loreto: "Here is the wonderful synthesis of all the shrines of the world."[13]

A house, be it a hut or a castle, is symbolic of the center of the universe, the Source and the goal of the human journey. St. Teresa wrote, "Consider our soul to be like a castle made entirely of diamond...in which there are many rooms....If this castle is the soul, *clearly one does not have to enter it since it is within oneself.* How foolish it would seem if we were to tell someone to enter a room he was already in."[14] This is a remarkably clear reference to the equivalence of the divine Source and the essential Self in us and in nature. What a contrast between the diamond soul of St. Teresa of Avila and our first introduction to the soul as stained by sin!

A house appearing in dreams is thought to represent the human psyche and body. Psychotherapist Ania Teillard says that in psychoanalysis, a house signifies the layers in the psyche. The exterior of the house represents our persona, our outward appearance—both our body and the personality we present to the world. The floors are the layers of consciousness in us and the stairs are the connections between them. The attic is our higher archetypal consciousness and the cellar is our roiling unconscious and instincts. The kitchen is the place where food is transformed by cooking so it can become a source of nurturance. This is an alchemical symbol of the changes we are capable of when our ego is burned away so the divine Source can work through us. The doors represent our openness to the world and our passages in and out. Through them, we move from contemplative silence to active work and universal charity.

This description from depth psychology is a richly spiritual view that shows how a house is an image carefully and usefully lodged in our consciousness. It shows us the dimensions and potentials of our true selves. As a title of Mary, a house serves that same purpose. She is the dwelling place of the human psyche in which the transformative mother is at work. Our task is to allow that work to happen no matter how hot the kitchen may become or how many stairs there are to climb. We are never alone in the house; our mother and our spiritual ancestors are at home with us as helpers and sponsors.

We find this reference to Solomon's temple, "He overlaid the whole house with gold, in order that the whole house might be perfect" (1 Kgs 6:22). At its dedication,

God promised to hear the prayers uttered in it. Mary, in this title, is honored as the archetype of the golden temple in whom prayers are surely heard.

Gold was common in ancient times since it did not require the use of metallurgy to process it for use. It is thus symbolic of our pure essential Self that does not require the interventions of ego. It is thereby also a symbol of grace and of spiritual virginity. Gold in India was called *mineral light*. Gilding of images of gods and saints was meant to show their spiritual perfection and how they hearken from a world beyond impermanence. Byzantine icons were gilded to reflect light from heaven, and halos are gold auras betokening divine light.

Images of gold appear throughout the Scriptures. In the Book of Revelation, the new Jerusalem is a symbol of spiritual wholeness since it was made by God as opposed to the transitory version made by man: "The wall is built of jasper, while the city is pure gold, clear as glass" (21:18). Gold is likewise a gift of the Magi, a gift of the wider world to Christ who is always embracing the entire cosmos from Mary's arms: "They saw the child with Mary his mother" (Matt 2:11).

Gold can also be tried or tested: "When he has tested me, I shall come out like gold" (Job 23:10). Thus, there is in this title, as we are seeing in all of them, a shadow side. Gold is associated with greed and miserliness. Gold can tempt us to sell our loyalty.

This House of Gold of the spiritual Self stands in contrast to the Golden House built by Nero, a personification of the ego, after the fire he set in Rome in AD 64. This was a house of vanity that was itself destroyed soon after. The persecuted Christians whose numbers increased would build a city of God in its place. After the conflagration of ego desire, comes the house of gold of real value, that is, of an essential truth. This is the necessarily painful chapter in the story of human transformation.

By the invocation *House of Gold*, we commit ourselves to enter the mansion of spiritual individuation. What happened to Mary can happen to us: we make a series of surrenders and choices that move us out into the world with treasures to share. This passage will have suffering in it and joy too, like all human enterprises that say yes to the inexorable conditions of existence. That yes to golden light and darkness too is what makes for wholeness.

Finally, we are aware that a cathedral is a container, a house of gold, a sacred space where God is always present and nourishing us in the Eucharist. A cathedral is thus the stone equivalent of Mary's body. This may be part of the reason that the builders of French cathedrals named them after her. The cosmos is also a container of all creation where mother nature is always present and nurturing us.

In the fire of creation,
Gold does not vanish:
The fire brightens.
Each creature God made
Must live in its own true nature;
How could I resist my nature,
That lives for oneness with God?
—St. Mechtild of Magdeburg,
The Flowing Light of the Godhead

Prayer

Mary, let me enter the house of your golden
   radiance.

May I find in you the virtues that make our world a
house of gold.
I share with you the house of earth and join you in
making it a palace of light.
I offer the sunrise and the sunset to you.
Help me in my beginnings and my endings.
Give me the strength to face new possibilities.
Give me the strength to face my griefs and trials.
I trust that I am always at home in your love and ask
to stay with you through all the seasons of my life.
May I help you make the world a house of golden love.
May I now grant hospitality to all those I have turned
away.
May I construct a mansion on earth that welcomes all
people.
May I ever include, never exclude.
Mary, you are my home and I am a home for you.
Thanks to you, no one and nothing is left outside.

ARK OF THE COVENANT

The grace of contemplation is rightly said to resemble the Ark. For just as in that Ark all the jewels and relics of the Temple were contained, in this little love, when it is offered, are contained all the virtues of the human soul, which is the temple of God.
—Anonymous fourteenth-century English mystic,
The Cloud of Unknowing

The ark is a container, hence a feminine symbol, this
time holding both masculine and feminine objects: "In it
stood the golden altar of incense and the ark of the
covenant overlaid on all sides with gold, in which there were

a golden urn holding the manna, and Aaron's rod that budded, and the tablets of the covenant" (Heb 9:4). The ark was made of incorruptible wood, a symbol of the deathless Self. As we noted earlier, the word *Shekinah* is the Hebrew word for the ark, connoting the feminine presence of God.

The ark of the covenant was the pledge of divine protection, so it was taken into battle. The ark is related in the Litany of Loreto to Mary's role as the mother who holds and preserves our intactness in the face of the threats of the inflated ego. The covenant is the promise that the ego can enter the service of the God-Self and be sanctified by it. When the Israelites fought without the ark in their ranks, they were defeated. This is an allegory of the need for grace (feminine energy) as a supplement to effort (masculine energy) in opening ourselves to the establishing of the ego/Self axis—union with God.

As the Israelites crossed the desert to the promised land, a cloud, signifying the presence of God, "overshadowed" the tent containing the ark. That same word is used in the annunciation story: "The Holy Spirit will come upon you, and the power of the Most High will overshadow you" (Luke 1:35). Mary contains Jesus in her womb as an ark. Likewise, she accompanies us as an ark of protection.

The ark provides a rich allegorical reference not only to Mary but, as with all the titles, to our universal destiny as humans. Jesus as Messiah is the personification and exemplar of our universal human calling to be present in the world creatively and redemptively.

Jesus is the Messiah who does not abrogate but fulfills the covenant. The images in the Litany, however, are out for higher stakes than to show how Christianity fulfills Judaism. They tell of how we are called to fulfill our cosmic evolutionary destiny to bring unconditional love, enlightened wisdom, and healing power into our world. It is not about preparation for a heaven in the future, but a commitment to a new heaven and a new earth here and now. In fact, this is why we are here now.

The three covenants of Judaism are those with Abraham, Noah, and Moses. The covenant with Abraham signifies the promise that God, the essential Self in all of us and in the cosmos, will remain alive in every generation. The covenant with Noah is that of the preservation of life until an omega point of evolution when a triumph of spirit will become visible in the material world. The covenant of Moses makes all of us a chosen race to bring the law of love to fruition. All three of these promises require masculine efforting and feminine containing for their fulfillment, hence the ark is such a rich image and symbol of Christ and Mary.

Hugh of St. Victor referred to the ark allegorically as the ark of the heart. It is the secret core of the body that is the equivalent of the Holy of Holies in the Temple of Jerusalem. It is the secret container of wholeness that awaits the gifts of divine grace and the work of human persever-ance to be released. The heart/ark is also the alchemical vessel in which the base metal of ego is transformed into the gold of the essential divine Self. In this context, it has been associated with a Christian counterpart, the Holy Grail, another symbol of wholeness. In the chalice, a natu-ral nutrient, wine, becomes the divine life force, redemp-tive blood. This depicts the shadow side of the image since suffering will be a necessary part of that process of trans-formation.

The Hymn for the Office of Our Lady of Lourdes shows the dark and light dimensions of the ark metaphor: "The torrent with its inauspicious waves which draws all men [egos] into the whirlpool, subsides into a placid sea [the divine Self] while the Ark of the covenant [feminine presence] is passing by." This is a reference to the dark red sea that awaited the Egyptian soldiers (the arrogant ego refusing rebirth) and dissolved them.

All these references are affirmations of the meaning Mary can have in our spiritual lives. We can see the titles in the Litany as pearls that have value singly but together create a stunning marvel of spiritual adornment and inner wealth. The invocations enrich us because they cull so many provocative metaphors about our spiritual path and what it takes to walk it.

"Then God's temple in heaven was opened, and the ark of his covenant was seen within his temple" (Rev 11:19). The ark is a heavenly figure since it is a container of the Divine. The personal ego world cannot hold such a tabernacle; only a transpersonal world can. The ark, like Mary herself, is transcendent and unlimited. In Ecclesiasticus, we read, "He that made me, rested in my tabernacle" (Sir 24:12).[15] This is why Saturday is Mary's day; God rested in her. She is the Sabbath, the feminine divine, and so are we when we grant hospitality to our feminine energies.

Meditation on a daily basis is conducive to releasing feminine energy. An account of creation in Exodus says, "On the seventh day he rested, and was refreshed" (31:17). The word, *nafash*, means "to rest or breathe," and *nefesh* is the human soul or spirit. Both these words are from the same root. So the breath of God is a metaphor for the soul at rest. The soul is feminine and so is the Sabbath of rest.

Since mindfulness meditation involves watching our breath, it is thus a direct contact with our untrammelled soul. In the Kabbalah, the highest level of the human soul is *neshamah*, the breath of God. The lowest level, the soul in us, is *nefesh* and what connects these is *ruach*, which means "breath" both as respiration and as the life force, the axis of the Divine and human soul. This is the meaning of Pentecost, an allegory of how the humbled ego becomes the mouthpiece of the good news. Mary sits in the Pentecost that keeps happening in every moment.

> *As the Ark arose, so on this day the virgin mother was taken up to her heavenly bridal chamber.*
> —Sermon of St. Anthony of Padua on the
> Feast of Mary's Assumption

Prayer

Mary you keep the divine life in safe-keeping for all of us.

You, not my ego, are my protection in times of conflict.

Let me dance in your presence.

Keep a covenant with me all my life.

You are here today accompanying me on my journey.

I feel your guidance and appreciate it.

Mary you contain all my past with its long history of light and dark.

You contain my present with its fears and longings.

You contain my future with its mystery and promise of endless life.

Hold all these in your heart.

Carry me in you as you carried Jesus.

Carry me as the ark carries the presence of God.

Be the Holy Grail to me, the wholeness of my mortal and immortal life that nourishes me in ever more marvelous ways.

May I be the presence of the Divine in my home, at
work, in the daily world, and in all that I do.
Like the cosmos, may I be a tabernacle of nourishing
and ever-evolving love.
Let me rest in you and awake in you.

GATE OF HEAVEN

*Look, I have set before you an open door, which no
one is able to shut.*

—Revelation 3:8

A gate or door is a symbol of a passage into a new
world or a new state of consciousness. Opening gates
means opening into a new world of grace. That knowledge
is the realization that what we believed in as literal all these
years was containing and preserving sacred metaphors
about the destiny and identity of ourselves and our world.
To walk through is to forsake literalism and polarity for a
courageous consciousness of who we really are. The Litany
of Loreto is a map of the far-flung and inner territories of
ourselves in the cosmos. We are those who pass through the
gate, and we are the gate through which revelation passes
to the world.

The divine feminine helps us cross the threshold. A
threshold is a crossroads of opposites; we are simultaneously in and out, familiar and alien, cosmos and chaos. It is
the liminal space in which we are nowhere and no one. To
be comfortable with such ambiguity requires a feminine
energy. At that point, a creative courage may come. Chaos
is after all, the prime matter—*material/mother*—of alchemical transformation, the stuff of creation and resurrection:

"The people who survived the sword / found grace in the wilderness" (Jer 31:2).

Myths about thresholds into new worlds include an animal or demon who tries to prevent our entry. At the temple gates are fierce guardians who indeed may frighten us. They demand a painful initiatory confrontation. The guardians of the gate are the shadow side of the givens of life that try our patience and our courage. They also symbolize entry into the unconscious, always a frightening prospect. In myths, it is usually the divine feminine who gives the hero a charm to pass by the threatening guards.

Through the gate, we pass from the profane world to the sacred world as happens when we enter a cathedral. Mary is the gate through which Jesus—Divine Consciousness —entered this world. Mary is the middle world gate through which we enter the sacred world of spiritual consciousness.

Christ is our exemplar of the human path to an incarnation of the Divine: "the firstborn within a large family" (Rom 8:29). To trust him when he says he is the door is to acknowledge that this transition is achieved not by human control but by grace. Jesus says, "Listen! I am standing at the door, knocking; if you hear my voice and open the door, I will come in to you and eat with you, and you with me" (Rev 3:20). This is the promise, to open the gate and let heaven enter earth.

For the Jews, Passover night was considered the time of the Messiah's arrival when the temple gates would open on their own. This is why the early Church expected the second coming on Easter eve, the new Passover, during which the faithful listened for a knock on the door. Only those who were ready—free of ego-fear and committed to

Christ's way—would be able to enter (cf. Rev 22:14 and Ps 118:20).

Mary, in the Gaelic litany, is called *Ladder of Heaven.* The title *Gate of Heaven* is taken from Genesis: "Surely the LORD is in this place—and I did not know it!...How awesome is this place! This is none other than the house of God, and this is the gate of heaven" (28:16–17). Jacob said this the morning after his vision of the ladder, connecting heaven and earth, that was trafficked by angels. The theme of ascent and descent, from ego to Self and Self to ego is likewise a covenant image. Access is always and everywhere available to our mortality so we can enter the divine life. That is the life that so zealously yearns to enter the mortal world.

Gold and precious metals represent spiritual meaning. In Herod's temple, the central gates were covered with gold and the "Beautiful Gate" was covered with brass. Here, while the gate was open, St. Peter cured a crippled man: "I have no silver or gold, but what I have I give you; in the name of Jesus Christ of Nazareth, stand up and walk" (Acts 3:6). An open gate is significant as a symbol of the entry into the temple of the divine Self. There is a touching and profoundly provocative legend that the parents of Mary, Joachim and Anne, met and fell in love at this same Beautiful Gate.

> *At the center of our being is a point of nothingness which is untouched by sin and by illusion, a point of pure truth, a point or spark which belongs entirely to God....This little point of nothingness and of absolute poverty is the pure glory of God in us....It is like a pure diamond, blazing with the invisible light of heaven. It is in everybody, and if we could see it we would see*

these billions of points of light coming together in the face and blaze of a sun that would make all the darkness and cruelty of life vanish completely...I have no program for this seeing. It is only given. But the gate of heaven is everywhere.

—Thomas Merton, *Conjectures of a Guilty Bystander*

Prayer

Mary help me see, open, and pass through the gate
between fear and love.
Show me every day how to reflect and foster compassion, wisdom, and healing.
Be a door for me into the divine life.
Help me say yes to the givens of human life.
May I accept how things change and end.
May I accept how things are not always fair.
May I accept how my best-laid plans may go wrong.
May I accept how that suffering is part of growth.
May I accept that people are sometimes hurtful
and disloyal
and may I never retaliate but instead pray for their
transformation.
Teach me to say yes to the givens of life as the will of
God.
Let me find in the givens the sources of compassion
for others.
Open the gate to your way of loving and seeing
where and how I can love more.
Open the gate to higher consciousness for me, Mary.
Open the gate and let the light through.
By your grace, may I be a gate of heaven on earth.

MORNING STAR

Until the day dawns and the morning star rises in your hearts.

—2 Peter 1:19

Morning is promise and beginning. The red morning star is a symbol of the rebirth of life, the homecoming of light. This connection to the theme of birth makes a star an apt symbol in the story of Bethlehem when it led the shepherds and the Magi to the infant Jesus.

The early Church fathers spoke of the "morning star" that shines brightly before the sun rises, as symbolic of Mary, the Mother of Jesus, the Light of the World—the Sun. The mystic, St. Bridget of Sweden, said of Mary, "She is the star that precedes the sun." Heavenly bodies, the stars, sun, and moon, are symbols of the spiritual dimensions of psyche, not earthbound, not ego-bound, but transcending us while at the same time hovering over us as our custodians.

The hymn for the Feast of the Rosary says, "Twelve stars now crown the brow of the glorious mother who reigns near the throne of her son over all created things." The stars in her crown are the beacon that calls us to the light. In the hymn for the feast of the guardian angels, Mary is called the *Mother of Light.*

Mary, reminiscent of the woman in the apocalypse, wears a crown of twelve stars, reminding us of the houses of the zodiac. She is thus the mother of all of us born under each and every sign. The stars refer to our destiny. The Great Mother is powerful over fate. We see this referred to in the Latin novel *The Golden Ass* when Apuleius prays to Isis: "O Holy Blessed Lady, constant comfort to humankind, your compassion nourishes us all. You care about those in trouble as a loving mother for her children. You are there when we call, stretching out your hand to push aside anything that might harm us. You even untangle the web of fate in which we may be caught, *even stopping the stars for us if their pattern is in any way harmful.*"[16] This pagan prayer is reminiscent of how we do not trust or ask Mary for all she wants to give us and our world. Our trust in the divine feminine is thereby still not in full bloom.

Our Lady of Light is a medieval title given to Mary by St. Thomas of Canterbury. That light is the light of new consciousness, the abundant potential in the higher Self once it is acknowledged by the ego, as sailors acknowledge the morning star with joy and a sense of being protected and guided. Such an image appears also in Shakespeare: "Look, the unfolding star calls up the shepherd."[17] The morning star was the signal to the shepherd to lead his sheep from the fold, that is, to begin another day of nurturing care.

The morning star is particularly associated with the sea. *Ave Maris Stella*, "Hail, Star of the Sea…Joyous Port of Heaven," is a ninth-century hymn with this same meaning. Pagan goddesses were associated with the primal waters. Even the Holy Spirit in the beginning of Genesis is depicted as a mother bird brooding over such waters. The great goddess Aphrodite is born of the sea. The Sumerian goddess who creates heaven and earth has a name that means sea. The name Mary in Latin, *Maria*, is a cognate of the word for sea, *maris*.

St. Ephraem wrote, "You are the only refuge of sinners and the safe harbor of those who are shipwrecked."[18] The divine feminine has a guiding quality that is available to all of us. An old Irish prayer says, "O Mary, meet me at the port." The complete Mary combines light and shadow. She can thus become a kind of port, providing a comfort that can stultify and an open sea that can become tempestuous. In Roman times, the guardian goddess, Isis, was portrayed with a ship. In tantric Buddhism, Tara is the Mother of all Buddhas and is known as the "mother of liberation." Tara ferries us across the river of samsara, the endless round of lifetimes, to the shore of nirvana, the final peace. Tara is called *the lady of the boats* who can calm the waves and floods. She goes out in boats with helper women to rescue those who are shipwrecked, that is, caught by ego-fears and desires. Tara says, "From the world ocean of many terrors I will save them." In this, we are reminded of the following address of Pericles to the raging heavens:

> O Divinest patroness, and midwife gentle
> To those that cry by night, convey thy deity
> Aboard our dancing boat....[19]

The Church is itself pictured as a ship that carries us over "life's tempestuous sea." This is why the word *nave* is used for the main aisle of a cathedral. The image implies protection and safety in the midst of change and upheaval. The eternal Self ferries the ego stably through its many vicissitudes on its voyage through the conditions of existence.

A number of years ago, I visited the childhood church of my grandmother in Meta di Sorrento, Italy, Our Lady of the Laurel. I noticed first a plaque that said it was built on the ruins of a temple of Minerva, goddess of wisdom, an indicator of the unity of the Great Mother archetype. Meta is a town on the water, and many of its citizens are sailors, my great-grandfather being one of them. In the church, I noticed a wall covered with many paintings of ships. Each of them was tossing perilously in the midst of nighttime storms. Each showed an image of Mary above the ship. She appeared as a shining starry light granting protection and assuring the sailors a safe passage through the convulsing waves. The images are a beautiful and touching example of the local people's appreciation of Mary as the Morning Star, a symbol of the Great Mother, the one trusted to show the way home. The old sailors did indeed trust the power of the divine feminine.

In Shakespeare's *The Tempest*, we read, "Though the seas threaten, they are merciful."[20] This is another reference to the dark side of the feminine. The Great Mother is the guide as well as the storm. The conditions of our human existence include threatening and dark seas. By faith, we trust, however, that within the same archetype is the mercy of a compassionate, luminous, and assuring presence. With this in mind, is it possible that the paintings in Grandma's church depicted Mary and the storm within one picture? *Perhaps the artists could not help but include both sides of Mary: storm and safety framed in one scene.* They loved her and that love made wholeness visible and a universal wisdom accessible to them, possibly without them even knowing it consciously.

> *Attired with stars, we shall forever sit,*
> *Triumphing over death, and chance, and thee O time.*
> —John Milton, "On Time"

Prayer

Mary, you are the promise and the compass for my
  human voyage.
Be a star on the sea of my life with all its many
  tempests.

Be a calming presence in the midst of the
tumultuous waves that often overtake me.
Let me see you both in the calming of the waves and
the rushing of the waves.
Let me trust your dark side that tries me and your
comforting side that cheers me.
May I be a light to those who are having a hard
voyage.
May I help those who are drowning in the waves of
greed, hate, and ignorance.
May I be a star not in the worldly ego's way but in a
spiritually guiding way.
Mary, radiate your light so that all fears may be
dispersed from every human heart.
You are the morning of our life and its evening.
And, most of all, I ask the Holy Spirit to give me
enough faith to trust you more and more.

HEALTH OF THE SICK

*Jesus went throughout Galilee, teaching in their syn-
agogues and proclaiming the good news of the kingdom and curing every disease and every sickness
among the people.*

—Matthew 4:23

Such healing power is a quality of the divine not only
in God but in all of us. It is associated with Mary as the
feminine aspect of the Divine, meaning that it is contained
in the feminine and available through the feminine by
grace. The Latin word for health is *salus,* which also means
"salvation." Health indicates spiritual salvation not just

physical wellness. We are always finding higher stakes in the spiritual world.

To say that Mary is the Health of the Sick is to say that nurturant love is a healing force. The veneration of Mary has led people throughout the centuries to feel this love in themselves and to dedicate themselves to healing. For example, St. Camillus, patron of the sick, founded an order to aid the ill precisely in honor of Our Lady, Health of the Sick. The life and work of St. Camillus in the seventeenth century provides a significant allegory. He was a soldier who was wounded in the leg, which never quite healed. Because of this disability, he was rejected for monastic life. St. Camillus did not despair. Instead, he devoted himself to caring for the sick. Later, he was ordained and founded his own congregation, the Ministers of the Sick. He and his followers worked in hospitals in Rome and Naples. St. Camillus attended to plague victims on ships arriving in Rome's harbor at Ostia. The first field medical unit was formed by St. Camillus when he sent men to serve the wounded in Hungary and Croatia. He was canonized in 1746 and is the patron of the sick and of nurses.

St. Camillus represents a crucial feature of the Christian message: the potential of grace to make our condition our calling. He himself was sickly most of his adult life, but that only served to make him more conscious of the needs of others who were suffering like himself. St. Camillus is a model of accepting the conditions of one's personal existence and thereby growing in Christlikeness. He was politicized as a champion of the neglected sick by his own incurable illness. This is how he was not a victim but a champion. His illness became the door to his destiny. In other words, both his illness and his charitable response arose from a divine Source.

The example of St. Camillus shows us that a calling is not just about giving to others from our store of gifts and talents. It is also about giving from our wounds. This is a way to befriend the shadow side so it can become a source of healing light. Our painful wounds become openings for us and for others too.

To say that Mary is the Health of the Sick is to say that we all contain the energy of the feminine archetype of healing. Sickness is not limited to its narrow literal meaning of physical illness. It means deficiency of any kind—our disabilities in loving, in talents, in vision are meant to be directions to our destiny of giving. We look at our deficiencies and feel compassion for others like us. We design an apostolate of works of mercy that are aimed at the people who are suffering as we are: If we are sick, we help the sick. If we are ignorant, we help the ignorant. If we are in an oppressed minority, we join our fellows in raising consciousness of equality for all.

Like St. Camillus, we do not wait but are always on the lookout for how we can do this. We go to the harbor, as it were, to see if anyone has the plague. We hear of war and send our prayers, our donations, or ourselves to heal the divisions that caused it. We commit ourselves to work for nonviolent solutions to problems both in our relationships and in the political sphere. Loving ourselves happens best when we do not avert our gaze from the suffering of others. This is because our willingness to see suffering engenders compassion, and that makes us loveable to ourselves.

We do all this with the help of grace. The title of Mary as *Health of the Sick* means that grace is what heals and we are its instruments. Mary showed us how at the annunciation when her surrender led to grace and her choice led to action. We say yes to our condition without protest or blame. We then find our purpose. That purpose is what we *are* in our deepest reality, full of graces. The graces are unconditional love in our hearts, wisdom in our minds, and healing power in our hands and souls. Grace is the source of wholeness.

The fact that herbs have healing power is an encouraging sign that the earth is with us in the enterprise of health. Nature, like Mary, is the Health of the Sick. "All is medicine" was a revelation to the Buddha as he contemplated the earth. That realization is the same as the one that says that all is divine or all is one. Mystical union is a way of affirming a coherence always and already in all that is. A moment of tender oneness with a person we love shows us the possibility in immediate palpable experience for this mystic realization. It is a short step from oneness with One to oneness with all. Such union is felt and known only in moments, as in Wordsworth's "a flash that has revealed/The invisible world."[21] Each invocation in the Litany of Loreto is just such a flash. Teilhard de Chardin remarked that truth has to appear in only one mind for one moment to become a universal phenomenon that "shall set everything ablaze!"[22]

The divine mother is the equivalent of this oceanic consciousness spoken of by mystics. Ramakrishna reports in his diary that once when he was close to suicide, he had a powerful and rescuing vision: "Suddenly the blessed Mother revealed Herself....And everything else vanished from my sight, leaving no trace whatsoever, and in their stead I saw a limitless, infinite, effulgent Ocean of Consciousness....As far as my eye could see, the shining billows were madly rushing at me from all sides...." Like all mystics, Ramakrishna gradually saw the Mother in everyone and in nature too: "Whatever is, is the Mother—isn't that so?"[23]

I visited Lourdes last year as a pilgrim. There, in front of the cave, I experienced something very special. I felt a spiritual vibration, a kind of spiritual presence there. And then in front of the image of the Virgin Mary, I prayed, I expressed my admiration for this holy place that has long been a source of inspiration and strength, that has provided spiritual solace, comfort, and healing to millions of people. And I prayed that this might continue for a long time to come.
—The Dalai Lama, *The Good Heart*

Prayer

Mary may my wounds become openings for a new
   way of loving and living.
Heal me of my blindness when I refuse to see the
   light.
Heal me of my deafness when I refuse to hear the
   good news.
Heal me of my muteness when I refuse to speak up
   against injustice.
Heal me of my lameness when I refuse to walk the
   path.
Be with me in physical illness so I can find healing.
Be with me in spiritual illness so I can find
   wholeness.
May I bring healing into the world in every way
   I can.
May I heal my relationships.
May I heal the environment.
May I heal divisions among people.
May I heal war and injustice.

May all that I am and will be bring healing to the
    world.
May I be open to accessing healing power by commit-
    ment to these four steps:
    Gratitude for grace
    Firm conscious intention to release healing energy
    Letting go of attachment to any particular
        outcome
    Saying "Thy will be done"[24]

REFUGE OF SINNERS

*The infinite goodness has such wide arms that it
takes whatever turns to it.*
                  —Dante, *The Divine Comedy*

Sin and repentance are corollaries of the archetypal
theme of redemption. Repentance is a return to the
Source, the God who is love and forgiveness. Repentance
does not mean discrediting or disparaging ourselves but
the joy of finding what really matters and fully connecting
to it. This includes forgiving ourselves. Forgiveness is letting go, handing ourselves and our sins over to God. Such
handing over is an antidote to any despair we might have
about ourselves and our lovability. Not to forgive ourselves
would mean not believing that God is love. Mary, Refuge of
Sinners, meets us where God is love.

The mystic Julian of Norwich, in her *Revelations of
Divine Love*, wrote, "Sin is befitting (useful or necessary),
but all shall be well."[25] She taught that sin has no ultimate
reality since it is based on ignorance and yet it does lead
to knowledge and thereby it is useful. This is a forceful way
to describe the shadow and its creative potential on our

spiritual journey. This potential is based on the certainty that there is no retaliation in God, only transformation. The mystery of the Divine is that *it makes all well in the end by never giving up on us.* To say that Mary is the refuge of sinners is to say that an energy of acceptance and forgiveness is always present in the divine feminine until the last moment of our life, no matter how we have disfigured it or despaired of it.

Mary is the refuge of sinners because we can trust the feminine energy in the psyche to show us the way to love and to repent when we have been unloving. Sins against others are deliberate breaks with the community of humankind. These happen by revenge, malice, greed, hate, and disrespect. Our calling is to love in turn by forgiving and reconciling rather than retaliating, by caring for others through the works of mercy, and by an unconditional self-giving. We are handing ourselves over to a higher power than the vindictive ego.

We might also break our connection to Mother Nature. She provides the warmth, nurturance, and beauty that is a sanctuary for us in our sorrows and confusion. It is sinful to disrespect nature and harm her with pollution and a misuse of her resources. We are asked to love the world by finding ways to preserve it, honor it, and amend our ways in it. This is the transition from sin, ego-aggrandizement, to unity, eco-aggrandizement.

Cardinal and theologian Henri de Lubac, in *Aspects of Buddhism*, said, "If I except the unique fact of the Incarnation, where we adore the trace and actual presence of God, Buddhism is probably the great spiritual event in history." Buddhism emphasizes the concept of refuges. In the Buddhist tradition, there are three refuges: the Buddha (enlightened mind), the Dharma (the teachings), and the

Sangha (the community of practitioners). These parallel the three refuges in Christianity: Christ, faith, and the Church. The Buddha mind is like Christ consciousness, a consciousness free of ego. The Dharma is the word of truth, Scripture, and Tradition that sets us free from ignorance. The Sangha is the community of believers we gather with, those who present the challenges and comforts so necessary on our spiritual path.

Sin means separation and *redemption* means reunion. St. Thomas Aquinas, in answer to the question about whether we can ever give up on ourselves, says that grace is always available no matter what we have done. Despair is therefore never truly necessary. We always have a refuge through the path of repentance.

Throughout childhood, we may have thought of Mary first when we felt we had done something terribly wrong. That was an intuitive recognition of what she stands for and what she offers us. Our faith-intuition told us that Mary does not give up on us ever. We always knew, deep down, how much she cares about our life and our destiny or how much she figures into it. Her divine feminine energy is the inner wholeness that urgently wants to fulfill itself in us and through us. That grace is the reason we do not give up on ourselves or others. If it all depended on us, we would be likely to give up more quickly and easily.

As we ponder the power of Mary in our lives, we see her standing under the star of Bethlehem that unites shepherds and kings. Mary stands under the cross and unites those who hurt and are hurt. Mary stands in the upper room on Pentecost and unites all humankind in the good news of salvation. She thus represents the feminine aspect of the Divine at moments at which redemption releases its most tender mercies.

Refuge of Sinners is one of the most comforting of all the titles in the Litany of Loreto since it combines the shadow of sin and the light of forgiveness. It thereby confirms the reality of a loving presence that is responsive to us when we are at our worst. We all make choices that are not in keeping with the love that is in us, not in keeping with the wisdom that is in us, not productive of the healing powers in us and through us. Such choices contradict the meaning of our humanity since that meaning is God, and God is the love we at times reject, the wisdom we at times disregard, and the healing we at times refuse to foster.

Sin is thus ultimately a disloyalty to the deepest reality of ourselves. It is going out of spiritual character. Calibrated into our psyche is a conscience that tells us when we have missed the mark—the many-splendored-life of God within us. In that same calibration is a simultaneous desire to make amends and to be forgiven. The archetype of Mary as the Refuge of Sinners stands in readiness for us in that moment.

Refuge means container and this title therefore certainly refers to Mary as a mother. To pray to Mary as Refuge of Sinners is not just a consolation; it is a way of noticing and honoring the transcendent mother who contains us unconditionally, both in sin and in grace. We do not have to measure up before she will love us; we measure up because she loves us.

In a way, any community in which we are loved and forgiven is a maternal container. Our experience in a supportive community shows us the nature of love: it has a motherly forgiving, all-including quality. We find that not only in Mary but in our own hearts every time we do not give up on ourselves or others. We accomplish this when we seek reconciliation rather than retribution in our relationships with others.

The Refuge of Sinners is not a place outside us but a home base always available to us on life's journey. Mary is the guide on our journey and is our homecoming.

I am the Queen of Heaven and the mother of mercy. I am the joy of the just, and the door through which sinners are brought to God. There is no sinner on earth so accursed as to be deprived of my mercy.
—Mary to St. Bridget of Sweden,
Celestial Revelations

Prayer

Mary, you help me let go of my shame about my limitations and mistakes.
You teach me how to ask for forgiveness and make amends.
Keep showing me the path to repentance and forgiveness.
I turn to you when I know I have done wrong.
You turn me to God's forgiveness.
You are always with me, loving me unconditionally, caring about my choices, helping me see more virtuous choices.
I am thankful for how I have felt your presence in times of error and ignorance.
May I learn to forgive myself.
May I be as forgiving to others as you are to me.
May I be a refuge to those who hurt me.
May they find a compassion in me that helps them change and grow.
May I love those who hate or hurt me and pray now and always for their conversion.

May I let retaliation change into reconciliation.
May I let hurt change into healing.
May I let fear change into love.

COMFORTER OF THE TROUBLED

Tell them that, to ease them of their griefs,
Their fears of hostile strokes, their aches, losses,
Their pangs of love, with other incident throes
That nature's fragile vessel doth sustain
In life's uncertain voyage, I will some kindness do them.
—Shakespeare, *Timon of Athens* (V.II)

A religious community in Spain was founded in 1380 to rescue abandoned children. It was called *The Mount of Pity* under the protection of The Mother of the Forsaken. To associate pity for children with the feminine archetype is natural. This is why a title like *Comforter of the Troubled* is applied to Mary and, therefore, to the feminine in us.

This title takes us to the core of the Christian gospel. Commitment to the good news is not about beliefs, or being right, or being preferred. It is about loving in the most practical and immediate ways. The call, the challenge, and the grace of a spiritual life is commitment to the works of mercy. The bodily works of mercy are to

Feed the hungry;
Give drink to the thirsty;
Clothe the naked;
Shelter the homeless;
Visit the sick and imprisoned; and
Assist the dying.

Today, with TV and the media informing us daily of human needs and suffering on a global scale, we are being given many opportunities to be Christ's mercy in the world. We see the deficiencies and horrors people face around the world, and we can choose to join or support organizations that help them or we can simply switch the channel. The choice is a commitment to acts of mercy or a disregard that permits the injustice to continue.

The spiritual works of mercy are to

Comfort the troubled;
Counsel the confused;
Provide information to those who need it;
Speak up to the unjust;
Forgive injuries;
Bear wrongs without retaliation; and
Pray for the living and the dead.

Each of these works of mercy is a challenge to undo some form of oppression. Redemption means release from injustices. In this sense, salvation is always and already happening as long as we are engaged in the works of mercy in the world. We join in the redemptive renewal when we see pain and respond to it with the forms of compassion outlined in the works of mercy.

Three stages may occur in our expression of the works of mercy. At first we are touched by the suffering of others; we wish the best for them and do not add to their suffering. In the second stage, we cultivate the mind of love, working out specific and ongoing ways to make a contribution to the well-being of others. In the final stage, we are dedicated to a life of universal love. This is commitment to sanctity. *Which stage am I in at this time in my life?*

Spiritual practice leads to developing the musculature to hold a wounded humanity as Mary does in Michelangelo's *Pietà*. Our work is to expand our lap and widen our embrace. Our trials in life and its conditions are a discipline, a workout to build this strength. We are children of Mary when her children are ours. That is the unifying love that makes us conscious of others' pain and makes us more apt to heal it. God is love means that we are love in the world. Each of us is called to show *how* God is love.

What does this look like in practical terms? We show unconditional love, patience, courage, and joy. Humility and equanimity help us acknowledge our occasional helplessness as we accept the things we cannot change or amend. Finally, compassion springs from a felt sense of our shared humanity and leads back to the works of mercy. We then create a new set of givens in human relating, those of paradise: love, caring, and generous responsiveness to suffering.

The dark side of being a helper and healer is the same for both this title and the next one. It has to do first with a helper's potential for enabling those in need to imagine themselves as unalterably victimized or incapacitated. Appropriate contributions on the other hand, both psychological and physical, are those that facilitate others in helping themselves. Another dimension of the shadow of helping is hierarchical attitudes; the helper can consider himself as above the one being helped. It helps to recall that all of us need assistance in some way at some time. When others need help, we are there for them. When we need help, we hope they are there for us. Compassion is not hierarchical in any way; it is a peer relationship. Real love does not oblige us or advance us. It opens us to our purpose and makes us all equal.

Mother Teresa was a model of comforting the afflicted. She found a way to remain personally centered and serene while at the same time fully feeling the anguish of others. She did this not by alternating between the extremes but by holding them both simultaneously. This is how she literally "held herself together." She held the leprous with respect, not disgust, because in the moment of looking at the sores, she was still in full contact with God, her loving Source. In fact, Harding notes that "Mother Teresa...solved the problem of being surrounded by unbearable suffering by immersion in it, by being it absolutely and not being it absolutely. It is not a case of balancing one thing against the other, of compromise or moderation, but of extremism."[26]

The mature spiritual path is the one that holds an entire spectrum of extremes. On the cross, Christ said, "Why have you forsaken me," *and*, "I commend my soul to you" in the same hour. This is a metaphor for a rich human possibility to hold the apparently opposing energies of our feeling selves. In traditional theology, Christ on earth was thought to be always simultaneously in the heavenly presence of God. This now outmoded belief is nonetheless a way of preserving a truth: we are always connected to the eternal no matter what the circumstances or distractions. That is part of sanctity—wholeness.

The saints are continually assisting and accompanying forces and models for us. They are benevolent and mighty collaborators who encircle us invisibly throughout the day and especially in times of crisis:

When [Elisha] rose early in the morning and went out, an army with horses and chariots was all around the city. His servant said, "Alas, master!

What shall we do?" He replied, "Do not be afraid, for there are more with us than there are with them." Then Elisha prayed: "O LORD, please open his eyes that he may see." So the LORD opened the eyes of the servant, and he saw; the mountain was full of horses and chariots of fire all around Elisha. (2 Kgs 6:15–17)

We admire certain saints more than others. There is a reason for this. It is because they represent and personify our own untapped potential. *The saints we most admire had and gave the very gifts that are in us too.* Our admiration of others is a clue to a cornucopia of gifts and possibilities in us. One way to know our apostolate in the world is to consider which saints, canonized or not, we most look up to. They are the ones to imitate and to invoke as patrons in finding and fulfilling our vocation. Admiration is part of discernment. It points to our life purpose, our destiny, and to our assisting forces ever visibly or invisibly surrounding us.

Let your steadfast love become my comfort
according to your promise to your servant.
—Psalm 119:76

Prayer

Comfort us all, grace-giving Mary, and let me join
you in comforting the world.
I commit myself to act with mercy in every way I can.
I will look for ways to feed the hungry, clothe the
naked, and shelter the homeless.
I commit myself to comfort the troubled.

I commit myself to counsel the confused.
I commit myself to speak truth.
I commit myself to speak up to the unjust.
I commit myself to forgive injuries.
I commit myself to bear wrongs without retaliation.
I commit myself to pray for the living and the dead.
May I find the courage to act as Jesus Christ would
    act here in my world toward every person who
    makes a claim upon my love.
May I find my calling by appreciating the saints.
May I be open to the graces that come through them
    to help me on my path.

HELP OF CHRISTIANS

*We, like the Mother of the World, become the
compassionate presence that can hold, with
tenderness, the rising and passing waves of
suffering.*

—Tara Brach, *Radical Acceptance*

It is said that Pope Pius V added this invocation to the
Litany after the battle of Lepanto in the sixteenth century,
but this is unlikely since it first appears after his time. Pope
Pius VII was arrested by Napoleon in 1808 and released in
Rome on May 24, 1814. On that same day in 1815, he insti-
tuted the Feast of Mary, Help of Christians. Years later, in
1868, St. John Bosco, founder of the Salesians, dedicated
the mother church of his congregation in Turin to Our
Lady, Help of Christians. Since then, the Salesians have
carried on the devotion.

The title *Help of Christians* can be extended to include
all humanity. Once nonviolence is a spiritual practice, we

no longer believe in victory as the triumph of one army over another. Victory happens when war is avoided and peaceful means are applied to conflicts. There are no enemies in Christ's world of love, a world that began for us during the Sermon on the Mount and never ends. Christianity is a social reversal in world history: violence has been replaced with nonviolence, greed with sharing, fear with love, and dogmatic slavery with the freedom of the children of God. As Italian social commentator Danilo Dolci, dubbed "the Gandhi of Sicily," said in a talk after a four-day fast, "By our nonviolent action we shall show that truth has its own strength."[27]

We are called to a revolutionary love, one that is nonviolent, nonretaliatory, and all-inclusive. Martin Luther King's philosophy of nonviolence described in his first book, *Stride toward Freedom,* outlines the following six pivotal principles of nonviolence:

1. Nonviolence is a way of life for courageous people.
   It is active nonviolent resistance to evil.
   It takes spiritual, mental, and emotional discipline.
2. Nonviolence seeks to win friendship and understanding.
   The end result of nonviolence is redemption and reconciliation.
   The purpose of nonviolence is the creation of the Beloved Community.
3. Nonviolence seeks to defeat injustice, not people.
   Nonviolence recognizes that evildoers are also victims and are not evil people.

The nonviolent resister seeks to defeat evil, not people.

4. Nonviolence holds that suffering can educate and transform.

Nonviolence accepts suffering without retaliation.

Unearned suffering is redemptive and has tremendously enlightening and transforming possibilities.

5. Nonviolence chooses love instead of hate.

Nonviolence resists violence of the spirit as well as the body.

Nonviolent love is spontaneous, unmotivated, unselfish, unconditional, and creative.

6. Nonviolence believes that the universe is on the side of justice.

The nonviolent resister has deep faith that justice will eventually win.

Nonviolence believes that God is a God of justice.[28]

Based on these principles, in our commitment to peace and justice, we are not acting against the grain but with it since redemptive suffering is built into nature, for example, in the death of a rabbit, a brood of eagles can live.

Most prisoners of war suffer for years in reaction to what was done to them. The Tibetan Lamas, after being tortured by the Chinese, were not afflicted later with post-traumatic stress syndrome. Their spiritual practice over the years prepared them for any predicament that might arise from the depths of the human shadow. Their devotion to their faith and their trust in karma made them impervious to torture, since they were free of blame, hate, and retaliation. The Christian martyrs, in their tranquility in the face of death, surely achieved that same spiritual victory over hate and ignorance. A spiritual practice of nonviolence thus contributes not only to our sanctity but to our sanity. The hero is not the person who conquers others but the one who unites and reconciles them. The heroic journey is an evolution from the solo operating style of the ego to fellowship and interdependence. Such respect for life is the foundation of adult love. Interdependence is the key to caring about others because our own self-interest becomes equal to the interests of others. Compassion becomes unconditional and universal in its reach. That is the reach of Mary as helper of all humanity.

The hero archetype can become so autonomous that it is only a self-congratulating inflated ego, the shadow side of heroism. Becoming saintly is not a ruggedly individual task but a systems task. It happens successfully only when individual will becomes invested in cooperative effort. That happens in concert with any of the many forces of nonviolence and nonretaliation around us.

On April 24 each year, a striking example of one of these forces has been evident in the action of the Armenian community in Los Angeles, which gives blood at the local blood bank to be used by any citizen, Armenian or Turk in commemoration of the holocaust that took place on that day in 1915. They *choose* to shed their blood as they once were forced to shed it. They give life to those who took it from them. This is a symbolic reversal of tyranny and hate in favor of generous giving. It is also an admirable example of choosing reconciliation over retaliation.

For the ancient Greeks, the hero was half human and half divine. This is a metaphorical way of describing the axis of a healthy human ego and the transcendent Self. The hero combines the effort of the ego, the assistance of allies, and grace from the spiritual Self. Aid from beyond—beyond the ego's limited skill and capacity—means that a new consciousness allows for a safe conduct across the trestle of conflict, endowing us at last with what was kept from us before, the riches of unconditional love, perennial wisdom, and healing power—the qualities of the Divine. This is why relationship with the Beloved within is so central to the heroic journey.

A universally revered icon is that of Our Lady of Perpetual Help. It depicts a pious legend that the child Jesus was visited by two angels of truth who showed him the instruments of his future—suffering and death. He was frightened and leaped into his mother's arms so quickly that one of his sandals began to fall off. Mary holds him in the safety of her embrace but does not dismiss the angels with the thorns and spear. In the picture, we notice that Jesus is held in such a way as to be able to see the givens of his life *and* still feel safe. Mary holds him/ourselves in a way that grants stability but does not deny the dark options in human reality. That makes the cradling experience in the icon a spiritual tableau, a yes to what is and a redemption through what is.

The feminine images in the Litany of Loreto are consoling and animating. They are invitations, ways of opening to grace. Something, we know not what, is always and everywhere lovingly at work; we know not how, but we do know why: so that we can release the abundant possibilities of love, wisdom, and healing that are in us and for which the world is waiting.

Prayer

Mary, thank you for providing an ever-present help to all of us.

Place us in the unconditional light as we join you in rescuing a world still lost in the darkness of retaliation and war.

Help us love the world both as it is and as it can be.

Hold us by the hand as we engage passionately in the restoration of the world to Jesus Christ.

You held Jesus when he was born and then again when he died.

Hold us all our lives and at the hour of our death. Our life story is in your arms.

Keep your eye on us as we look into the face of danger and evil.

Make us the heroes and heroines who find ways to cocreate a world of harmony.

Be our Lady of victory over war and ego-division.

Be our support in bringing help to all those who need us no matter how different, unappealing, oppositional, or distant.

Be our loving guide in ending divisions among religions.

May we gather together under your mantle of compassion with only one prayer: that we may be one in love.

Mary, join me in commandeering to your love all those still standing at the gate, afraid to come into Christ's kingdom of commitment to peace and love.

Be, over and over, a help to all humanity.

We need you now more than ever.

Every gun that is made, every warship launched, every rocket fired signifies, in the final sense, a theft from those who hunger and are not fed, those who are cold and are not clothed.

—Dwight D. Eisenhower,
"The Chance for Peace,"
An Address to the American Society of
Newspaper Editors, 1953

Conclusion

A Cosmic Calling

> The ultimate vocation of the human race
> is in fact one, and divine.
>
> —Second Vatican Council, *Gaudium et Spes* 22

The word *calling* is often applied to personal careers. Our Christian calling has a world-embracing bigness. Richard Rohr writes, "The process of the divinization of human persons, or *theosis*, is for me at the very heart of the meaning of the Christian message."[1] We are drawn by a voice that beckons us to embody the Divine—just what Jesus did in his incarnation. The call is from within since God is precisely the More Within, the depth of our psychic life and of the cosmos.

To say that we honor the archetype of Mary within ourselves shows us three sides of our cosmic calling. They reflect the first titles of Mary in the Litany of Loreto: we are called to be intact/whole in honor of her virginity, nurturing of others in honor of her motherhood, and powerful in effecting world change in honor of her queenship. This calling includes a political consciousness infused with compassionate action—expressed in whatever way is right for us. We move beyond parochial or national concerns to cosmic ones. We are working for the world not just for our immediate citizenry. This is a clear and encouraging sign that we are being guided in the evolutionary process by hearts that have a universal expanse.

The invocations in the Litany are bugle calls that rally our soul to just such a cosmic calling. Some blow taps to ego-fears and attachments; some blow reveille to the heart that is ready to awaken. Each title is a soundbite that launches us on a journey of prayer, devotion, and imagery toward spiritual awakening, charitable action, and mystical union—our destiny on earth as it is in heaven.

These invocations have the power to enlighten, encourage, console, disturb, and dare. They accompany us and feed our soul, calling us to rise to our full spiritual stature. The Litany reflects the feminine divine as it attempts to describe its own magnitude—and that of our own souls.

A calling is a gripping incentive to invest our ego into the service of higher consciousness. In other words, our human limitations are upgraded when they are humbly surrendered to a higher purpose than the ego's favorite sports: fear, attachment, greed, retaliation, and control. We then can hear the inner and irrepressible call to be whole. Until then, there abides in us an ineradicable longing to fulfill our evolutionary destiny and thereby complete the program for which our unique personality was designed. When we still hold onto the egotistical way of living rather than follow the Sermon on the Mount, we are not fully ourselves. We are also not fully converted to Christianity. It is as if some sectors of our inner landscape have still not been missionized!

Alchemy can occur whereby the leaden ego is transmuted into the gold of the higher Self. Our ego and our body are the instruments of the divine work of peace and compassion on earth. We combine surrender and choice—the two responses of Mary at the annunciation. It is a deft interplay of the impregnating Spirit at the annunciation and the encouraging Spirit of Pentecost. We stay to be filled with God and we go to fill the world with God.

The timing of the journey from individual ego-centeredness to cosmic consciousness is unique in every individual. There is a time for sitting on board the ship and waiting for the wind of grace and a time for turning the wheel with all our effort. The time spiritual progress takes is not within ego control but resides in a force greater than ego yet ever accompanying it as the angel Raphael accompanied Tobias with just the right healing balm at just the right time.

The ambition of God for us is probably far greater than any of the ambitions we have for ourselves. Our calling was never anything less than the whole life of Jesus and Mary from the annunciation to the ascension and assumption. The images we venerated were not icons but *mirrors* of our inner life: a heart on the outside beaming love in every direction, a virgin pregnant with God, bread that can nourish the world, an empty tomb that opens to the light.

My calling is ultimately to name myself in many more ways than one. My physical origins reveal my ego identity. At the same time, my intrinsic nature is the essential being of the universe. My existential body has a size that can be changed by diet and exercise. My essence is pure light and nothing can change it. I am of double parentage: Louise, my mother here and Mary, my mother Here/Hereafter. This is what Jesus meant by, "Rejoice that your names are written in heaven" (Luke 10:20). From now on, I will have to give my full location and identity, not found on my driver's license, if the angels are to find me.

Finally, I share a personal experience that describes the essence of the Christian calling. One day in Venice, in the church of San Zaccaria, I was gazing at a painting of the Madonna and Child by Giovanni Bellini. A priest was leading a small congregation in the Litany of Loreto. I was following the titles, and when the priest came to the final title, I was surprised to hear him add one: *Capolavoro della Carita*, which means "Masterpiece of Love." I was awestruck by those words. I felt the utter rightness of this title, which struck me deeply and personally. Suddenly, by a grace, I could *feel* the love of Mary for me and my love for her in one instant. I kept looking at the Bellini painting and realized that he must have felt it too and was inspired to create the luminous work. I then realized that Mary wanted to paint me to look like her Son and that all of us were meant to be her masterpiece. This was always her intention and her promise.

Then grace opened my heart in yet another way and I felt a clearer kinship to Mother Nature and understood that this universe is *her* masterpiece, meant to be protected and honored like the painting above my head. I understood with a certainty that nature and the Divine and the human are indeed all one. I also knew that Mary is indeed the masterpiece of God, preserved by the Church for so many centuries, preserved by humanity for so many ages. I know my wonder will never be expansive enough to appreciate the unfathomable meaning of such a gift to humanity. "Imagine being given a mother like this one!" I thought. How loved we must be. Love must be our divine calling and our response to this cosmic calling will be *our* masterpiece.

> *May I show all the love I have*
> *In any way I can*
> *Here, now, and all the time,*
> *To everything and everyone—including me,*
> *Since love is what we are—and why.*
> *Now nothing matters more*
> *Or gives me greater joy.*

The Litany of Loreto

Lord, have mercy on us.
Christ have mercy on us.
Lord, have mercy on us.

Christ, hear us. Christ graciously hear us.
God, the Father of heaven, have mercy on us.
God the Son, Redeemer of the world, have mercy
    on us.
God the Holy Spirit, have mercy on us.

Holy Trinity, one God, have mercy on us.
Holy Mary, pray for us.
Holy Mother of God, pray for us.
Holy Virgin of virgins, pray for us.

Mother of Christ, pray for us.
Mother of divine grace, pray for us.
Mother most pure, pray for us.
Mother most chaste, pray for us.
Mother inviolate, pray for us.
Mother undefiled, pray for us.
Mother most amiable, pray for us.
Mother most admirable, pray for us.

Mother of good counsel, pray for us.
Mother of our Creator, pray for us.
Mother of our Savior, pray for us.

Virgin most prudent, pray for us.
Virgin most venerable, pray for us.
Virgin most renowned, pray for us.
Virgin most powerful, pray for us.
Virgin most merciful, pray for us.
Virgin most faithful, pray for us.

Mirror of justice, pray for us.
Seat of wisdom, pray for us.
Cause of our joy, pray for us.
Spiritual vessel, pray for us.
Vessel of honor, pray for us.
Singular vessel of devotion, pray for us.
Mystical rose, pray for us.
Tower of David, pray for us.
Tower of ivory, pray for us.
House of gold, pray for us.
Ark of the Covenant, pray for us.
Gate of heaven, pray for us.
Morning star, pray for us.
Health of the sick, pray for us.
Refuge of sinners, pray for us.
Comforter of the afflicted, pray for us.
Help of Christians, pray for us.

Queen of Angels, pray for us.
Queen of Patriarchs, pray for us.
Queen of Prophets, pray for us.
Queen of Apostles, pray for us.

Queen of Martyrs, pray for us.
Queen of Confessors, pray for us.
Queen of Virgins, pray for us.
Queen of all Saints, pray for us.
Queen conceived without original sin, pray for us.
Queen assumed into heaven, pray for us.
Queen of the most holy Rosary, pray for us.
Queen of Peace, pray for us.

Lamb of God, who takes away the sins of the world,
spare us, O Lord.
Lamb of God, who takes away the sins of the world,
graciously hear us, O Lord.
Lamb of God, who takes away the sins of the world,
have mercy on us.

V. Pray for us, O holy Mother of God.
R. That we may be made worthy of the promises of
   Christ.

Let Us Pray:
Grant, O Lord God, that we, Your servants, may
   rejoice in continual health of mind and body; and,
   by the glorious intercession of the Blessed Mary
   ever Virgin, may be delivered from present
   sadness, and enter into the joy of Your eternal
   gladness.
Through Christ our Lord. Amen.

A Retreat with Mary

Let us look to Our Lady, the woman of blessed hope, let us learn from her, let us pray to her, let us follow her, because she points and guides to Jesus her son as the light of the world, the way, the truth and the life. She is the dawn and the morning star, announcing the rising sun. She is accompanying us, helping us, guiding us, encouraging us to what Jesus prayed for and left us as his testament: that all be one.

—Cardinal Walter Kasper, "Mary and the Unity
of the Church" Ecumenical Conference, 2008
(*note the use of images from the Litany of Loreto*)

You may want to make a retreat on your own or with others using sections of this book. As a suggestion, begin each day praying the Litany of Loreto, then contemplate and reflect on one or more titles in chapter 3 (three titles) and chapter 4 (seventeen titles). Read the text meditatively, and end with the prayer that follows the text. Recite the prayer in the text once or more each day, for example, in the morning and/or before going to bed. A personal prayer/retreat upgrades the reading of this book from informative to contemplative, and the reader becomes more like Mary who "treasured all these words and pondered them in her heart" (Luke 2:19). Use the suggestions that follow as points of departure that may foster what you find meaningful in prayer. Find ways to turn each prayer into a practice in the world. We can pray by affirmation, writing, art, movement, dance, music, action, silence, responsiveness to nature, intimate love, interpersonal sharing, peeling garlic, anything at all.

Here are some spiritual and imaginative practices that help us enter more fully into the treasury of images in the Litany of Loreto:

Work with an image directly. The word *compose* comes from Latin words meaning "to place together." In art, composition is crucial to the experience of beauty. We respond to words and their inherent images by composing them with our life experiences and by composing our own words around them, like bees around a rose. For instance, if we are facing a question and require discernment, we may pray to Our Lady as Seat of Wisdom while also picturing her as a guide in our hearts inspiring us with her wisdom about what is happening in our lives.

Use this four-step process for imaging:

1. Imagine a picture that arises from a title in the Litany.
2. Explore your own psychological inner feeling space, for example, your past, your memories of Mary's place in your life, and how she can assist you now as she has before.
3. Find the symbolic level by engaging a mythic, cosmic sense of continuity with all our ancestors of faith who have prayed to Mary under this title.

4. Notice a shift as the doors of perception open to a direct experiential vision without the need for images. Intuition and mysticism begins here.

Images affect and are affected by physical reactions. Images generate similar internal responses as the actual stimuli. Images are the bridges between the conscious processing of information and physical changes, influencing both the voluntary and involuntary nervous system. For example, imagine the morning star or a destructive storm and notice your resultant tranquility or panic. An image also includes not only a picture but the way we experience it, *a felt sense.*

What is the felt sense in you that is stirred by the title you have been moved by?

Be aware that all those who felt this way and feel this way and pray this way are with you now in the communion of saints.

Notice new titles for Mary that arise in your consciousness. They are most likely based on what you need as graces and resources in the here and now. Images come to you like stars rising in the night sky. When you begin to see your images as visiting realities, not as things you think up, they become your inspiration and may even point to your calling.

Write your own litany to Mary based on what results.

Try writing a poem in response to a title that particularly appeals to you.

The Litany of Loreto contains not only words but silences. Pay attention to the spaces between the titles. They are the fertile silences that may speak to your condition as eloquently as the words. A Christian parallel to Buddhist mindfulness is "the prayer of simple regard" in which we look at something, for example, in nature, with no interpretation or interfering mindsets (fear, desire, judgment, expectation, and so on). Take a deep breath and simply witness the reality before your eyes while letting it speak to you as a revelation from God. This is a way of contacting the lightness of being, finding the transpersonal in the natural. It is indeed a mystical connection between the human, the Divine, and the natural. We look at an "it" and it becomes an "I," as Jesus encouraged us: "Be not afraid, it is I."

> Hail to you generous, glorious, and whole maiden...
> you are the base material of sanctity, the joy of God.
> All the blessings of heaven flowed into you
> and the Word became flesh in you.
> God looked at you before he created anything
> and he saw you as a white lily....
> In your womb was delight itself.
> A heavenly symphony resounded through you.
> Your purity became translucent with God.
> Your body was filled with bliss
> like grass inundated with the dew
> that brings out its greenness,
> O Mother of all joys.
> Let all the Church burst out in ecstasy
> in one cosmic symphony of praise
> to the sweet Virgin Mary
> Mother of God.

—Hildegaard of Bingen,
"Ave Generosa" in *Symphonia*

Notes

INTRODUCTION

1. Thomas Merton, *Thomas Merton: I have Seen What I Was Looking For, Selected Spiritual Writings*, ed. M. Basil Pennington (New York: New City Press, 2005), 94.

2. Emily Dickinson, "By a departing light," in *The Complete Poems of Emily Dickinson* (New York: Little Brown and Co., 1961), 1714.

CHAPTER ONE

1. Cf. David Richo, *How to Be an Adult in Faith and Spirituality* (Mahwah, NJ: Paulist Press, 2011).

CHAPTER TWO

1. Johann Wolfgang von Goethe, *Faust,* (F, 12110-11). See: Helga Druxes, *The Feminization of Dr. Faustus* (University Park, PA: The Pennsylvania State University, 1993), 2.

2. Pierre Teilhard de Chardin, *The Heart of Matter* (New York: William Collins Sons Co. Ltd. and Harcourt, Inc., 1978), 130.

3. Cynewulf, *Cynewulf's Christ: An Eighth Century Epic*, ed. Israel Gollancz (London: David Nutt, 1892), 25.

4. Wallace Stevens, *Notes toward A Supreme Fiction* (Omaha: The Cummington Press, 1942), VII.

CHAPTER THREE

1. Edmund Waterton, *Pietas Mariana Britannica: A History of English Devotion to the Most Blessed Virgin Marye Mother of God* (London: St. Joseph's Catholic Library, 1879), 169.

2. C. G. Jung, "On the Relation of Analytical Psychology to Poetry (1922)," in *The Spirit in Man, Art, and Literature*, vol. 15, *Collected Works of C.G. Jung* (Princeton, NJ: Princeton University Press, 1971), 82.

3. St. Ambrose of Milan, *Exposition of the Holy Gospel According to Saint Luke*, trans. Theodosia Tomkinson (Etna, CA: Center for Traditionalist Orthodox Studies, 1998).

4. Radcliffe G. Edmonds III, *Myths of the Underworld Journey* (New York: Cambridge University Press, 2012), 88.

5. Riane Eisler, *The Chalice and the Blade* (San Francisco: HarperOne, 1988), 101.

6. St. Bonaventure, "Mary as Queen" from the Third Nocturn of Matins, Lesson VII for the feast of the Queenship of Mary, http://www.rosarychurch.net/mary/queen3.html.

CHAPTER FOUR

1. Carl G. Jung, *The Portable Jung*, ed. Joseph Campbell (New York: Penguin Books, 1976), 648; cf. C. G. Jung, *Answer to Job*, vol. 11, *The Collected Works* (Princeton: Princeton University Press, 2010).

2. Apuleius, *The Golden Ass*, trans. Robert Graves (New York: Farrar, Straus and Giroux, 2009), 283.

3. Cf. The Poor Clares, Galway, *Calm the Soul* (Dublin: Hachette UK, 2014).

4. Cf. *Theosophical Quarterly*, vols. 18–19, 380.

5. Chogyam Trungpa and Francesca Fremantle, *The Tibetan Book of the Dead* (Boston, MA: Shambhala Publications, 2000), 95.

6. Cf. New Oxford Annotated Bible.

7. Mechtild of Magdeburg, *The Flowing Light of the Godhead*; Cf. Matthew Fox, *Meister Eckhart: A Mystic Warrior for Our Times* (Novato, CA: New World Library, 2014), 85.

8. C. G. Jung, *Jung on Christianity*, ed. Murray Stein, (Princeton, NJ: Princeton University Press, 1999), 251, 252.

9. C. G. Jung, *Answer to Job* (Princeton, NJ: Princeton University Press, 2010), 100.

10. Edward Schillebeeckx, *Jesus: An Experiment in Christology* (New York: Crossroad, 1987), 202.

11. Roman Missal: Rite for the blessing of baptismal water on Holy Saturday.

12. Pierre Teilhard de Chardin, "The Mass on the World," in *The Heart of Matter* (New York: Harcourt Brace Jovanovich, 1978), 24.

13. See http://www.catholictradition.org/Mary/loreto 3b.htm.

14. St. Teresa of Avila, *The Interior Castle: Study Edition*, eds. Kieran Kavanaugh, OCD, and Carol Lisi, OCDS (Washington, DC: Institute of Carmelite Studies, 2010).

15. Douay-Rheims 1899 American Edition.

16. Apuleius, *The Golden Ass*, trans. Robert Graves (New York: Farrar, Straus and Giroux, 2009), 283. See, also, Robert J. Karris, OFM, *A Symphony of New Testament Hymns* (Collegeville, MN: Liturgical Press, 1996), 178.

17. William Shakespeare, *Measure for Measure*, Act IV, Scene II.

18. St. Ephraem the Syrian (306–373), *The Essential Mary Handbook*, ed. Judith A. Bauer (Liguori, MO: Liguori Publications, 1999), 111.

19. William Shakespeare, *Pericles*, Act III, Scene I.

20. William Shakespeare, *The Tempest*, Act V, Scene I.

21. William Wordsworth, "The Prelude," Book 6, 601–2.

22. Pierre Teilhard de Chardin, *Le Christique* (Unpublished, 1955).

23. Paramahansa Ramakrishna in Nikhilananda, Swami, trans., *The Gospel of Sri Ramakrishna* (New York: Ramakrishna-Vivekananda Center, 1978), c1942, 14ff. Cf. also, http://goldenageofgaia.com/spiritual-essays/the-nature-of-the-divine-mother/the-divine-mother-is-all-we-can-know/.

24. These are four powerful steps toward opening ourselves to the healing possibilities in us both spiritually and physically. Healing biophotons can be emitted from our hands. Conscious intention, as in the four steps, is causal and nonlocal. According to recent discoveries in science, this may be how healing happens even through prayer at a distance. In the quantum world, there are no barriers of distance, as in the mystical world we contact in devotion.

25. Julian of Norwich, *Revelations of Divine Love* (New York: Penguin Books, 1999), Thirteenth Revelation, chapter 27, 79.

26. Douglas Edison Harding, *Head Off Stress* (London: The Shollond Trust, 2009).

27. Jerre Mangione, *A Passion for Sicilians: The World around Danilo Dolci* (New York: William Morrow, 1968), 84.

28. See more at http://www.thekingcenter.org/king-philosophy#sub2.

CONCLUSION

1. Richard Rohr, *Falling Upwards* (Hoboken, NJ: Jossey-Bass, 2011), 173.

Other Paulist Press Titles by the Author

How to Be an Adult: A Handbook on Psychological and Spiritual Integration (Paulist Press, 1991) explores how we can evolve from the neurotic ego through a healthy ego to the spiritual Self so that we can deal with fear, anger, and guilt. It offers ways that we can be assertive, have boundaries, and build intimacy.

How to Be an Adult in Faith and Spirituality (Paulist Press, 2011) explores and compares religion and spirituality with an emphasis on how they can both become rich resources for personal growth. We increase our understanding of God, faith, and life's plaguing questions in the light of mysticism, depth psychology, and our new appreciation of evolutionary cosmology.

How to Be an Adult in Faith and Spirituality (Paulist Press, 2012, compact disc). This set of four CDs is compiled from a workshop given at Spirit Rock Retreat Center in California on how to design and practice an adult spirituality. They examine the spiritual riches in religion and how to discern what is not in keeping with our adult evolution.

The Sacred Heart of the World: Restoring Mystical Devotion to Our Spiritual Life (Paulist Press, 2007) explores the symbolism of the heart in world religious traditions and, then, traces the historical thread of Christian devotion to the Sacred Heart of Jesus into modern times. The book focuses on the philosophy and theology of Teilhard de Chardin and Karl Rahner to design a new sense of what devotion can be.

When Catholic Means Cosmic: Opening to a Big-Hearted Faith (Paulist Press, 2015) explores the impact of a cosmic dimension of our faith: when our faith becomes a trust without limit, our hope overflows with expectancy and our love stretches beyond all barriers. The book notes how our spirituality expands as we update our beliefs in accord with the best advances in psychology and science.

When Love Meets Fear: Becoming Defense-less and Resource-full (Paulist, 1997). Our lively energy is inhibited by fear and we are so often needlessly on the defensive. This book considers the origins and healings of our fears of closeness, commitment, aloneness, assertiveness, and panic attacks so that we can free ourselves from the grip of fear that stops or drives us.

Other Titles by the Author

Being True to Life: Poetic Paths to Personal Growth (Shambhala, 2009)

Coming Home to Who You Are: Discovering Your Natural Capacity for Love, Integrity, and Compassion (Shambhala, 2012)

Daring to Trust: Opening Ourselves to Real Love and Intimacy (Shambhala, 2010)

The Five Things We Cannot Change and the Happiness We Find by Embracing Them (Shambhala, 2005)

How to be an Adult in Love: Letting Love in Safely and Showing It Recklessly (Shambhala, 2013)

How To Be An Adult in Relationships: The Five Keys to Mindful Loving (Shambhala, 2002)

Mary Within Us: A Jungian Contemplation of Her Titles & Powers (Human Development Books, 2007)

The Power of Coincidence: How Life Shows Us What We Need to Know (Shambhala, 2007)

The Power of Grace: Recognizing Unexpected Gifts on the Path (Shambhala, 2014)

Shadow Dance: Liberating the Power and Creativity of Your Dark Side (Shambhala, 1999)

When the Past Is Present: Healing the Emotional Wounds That Sabotage Our Relationships (Shambhala, 2008)

Wisdom's Way: Quotations for Meditation (Human Development Books, 2008)

You Are Not What You Think: The Egoless Path to Self-Esteem and Generous Love (Shambhala, 2015)